Pierre-Sylvain Filliozat

The Sanskrit Language: an Overview

History and structure, linguistic and philosophical representations, uses and users

Translated from the French by
T.K. Gopalan

INDICA

Cover illustration: Sanskrit manuscript of *Yoga Vāsiha Sāra*

Original title: *Le Sanskrit*
Collection *Que sais-je?* n° 1416

1st English edition: 2000
2nd English edition: 2009

Indica Books
D 40/18 Godowlia
Varanasi - 221 001 (U.P.)
India
E-mail : indicabooks@satyam.net.in
indicabooks@indicabooks.com

ISBN: 81-86569-17-0

Published with the assistance of
the Cultural Section of the Embassy of France in India

Acknowledgements of the Translator:
I am grateful, among several friends, to Dr. V. Kameswari, and especially to T.V. Vasudeva, of the Kuppuswamy Sastri Research Institute, Chennai, for helping with the citations in Chapters 1 and 2, to T. Jayaraman of the Government Arts College, Mannargudi for exhaustively going through the initial draft of the translation and offering numerous critical comments, to Professor P.-S. Filliozat for reading both the initial and the subsequent drafts and clearing my doubts and to Dominik Wujastyk of the Wellcome Institute for the History of Medicine, London, for going through the final version with meticulous care and suggesting a number of corrections, and for providing an original translation of the passage from Caraka figuring in chapter 3.

T.K. Gopalan

Printed in India by
First Impression New India
011-22481754, 09811224048

CONTENTS

INTRODUCTION

Few languages have had as remarkable a destiny as Sanskrit. It is remarkable first by its longevity. Only Chinese can compare with it in age; for, while Chinese does not have literary monuments as great as the Vedas for the ancient period, it is a language of very great vitality today. Sanskrit is also remarkable in the stability of its form during the course of history. It differs in this respect from Chinese which has changed considerably during the ages. Lastly, and this is perhaps its most original feature, Sanskrit has been elevated to the level of a sacred language, more than any other language. Any description of Sanskrit must necessarily bring to light and try to explain these three features: longevity, stability, sacredness. They are not natural features of language. They are effects of the action of the users of the language. Who are the users? And how did they use it? It is by contemplating these questions that explanations may be found for the nature and originality of Sanskrit.

From early antiquity speakers of Sanskrit reflected on their own speech. All language exists as a knowledge as well as a state of awareness in the minds of individual speakers. It is important to describe this state of awareness, or in other words what the speaker knows about his language. In the case of Sanskrit we are very well informed about it. Well-read Indians, with very keen linguistic awareness, have taken care to formulate how they represented their spoken language to themselves. This representation is an integral part of the language, as a component of the conscious linguistic knowledge of the speaker.

The historical and comparative approach to languages is, as we know, chiefly a revolution of the nineteenth century. It is barely discernible in ancient India. We find traces of it in the mediaeval period. It develops with the coming of the modern age. But it is never a decisive component in the linguistic awareness of the Sanskrit men of letters. Some of the structures of Sanskrit revealed by historical and comparative grammar were unknown even to the most observant among speakers and the lettered. We must therefore describe Sanskrit from these two points of view: what the speakers knew about their language, and what they did not, namely, in broad terms the history of the language and its relationship with others, foreign and unknown to the speaker.

A language is a well-ordered system which functions by itself. A speaker with no particular linguistic awareness beyond the competence he has inherited speaks it very well and spontaneously so. A learned speaker acts differently, does not let himself be influenced to the same degree by the system of his language, but, by the way he views it, can direct its use into different directions, and intentionally adapt it to new uses. Lastly he can also contain it in the system which he attributes to it and prevent it from evolving spontaneously. What is certain is that the Sanskrit men of letters profoundly influenced their language. Sanskrit has been preserved and at the same time reshaped more than any other language. It is important to define this third aspect.

Sanskrit at first evolved spontaneously. Then there has been a long period of gestation of linguistic awareness. Thereafter, and only after the Christian era, has there been a reaction of the effects of this awareness on the language, which is often called its stabilisation. We shall see below the deeper meaning of the word 'Sanskrit', and also that the language was so named only after the Christian era, in reference to the evolved form whose model has been conditioned by the views of the grammarians. By a retrospective extension it is also used for the archaic form which is the language of the Veda. We shall distinguish between the two forms, when it is necessary to be more specific, by using 'Vedic Sanskrit' or 'Vedic' for the old form and 'Classical Sanskrit' for the post-Patañjalian form.

Note on the pronunciation of the Sanskrit words

Sanskrit clearly distinguishes between short and long vowels, the long vowels being pronounced for twice as long as the short vowels and indicated here by a macron written on top of the roman letter: *ā ī ū*

e and *o* are always long.

u is pronounced as *u* in [put].

e is pronounced as *e* in *café* (but longer).

ai and *au* are diphthongs which are pronounced respectively *a-i* and *a-u*.

ṛ and *ḷ* are vowels and are pronounced approximately *ri* and *li*.

The consonants followed by a *h* are strongly aspirated.

c is pronounced as ch in [church].

j is pronounced as j in [judge].

The consonants marked with a dot below are retroflex pronounced by rolling the tongue backwards so that its tip points to the back of the palate.

r is rolled with the tip of the tongue.

ś is close to the German *ch* in *ich*, or to the *sh* in *Shakespeare*

ṣ is close to the French *ch*, without rounding of the lips.

s is voiceless, is always pronounced as in *hiss* never as in *easy*.

h is strongly aspirated.

ṃ is pronounced by nasalising the preceding vowel and by following it with the sound *m*.

ḥ is a voiceless aspirate which is pronounced in practice by making an echo of the preceding vowel with a light aspiration: *rāmaḥ* is pronounced *rāma-ha*, *hariḥ hari-hi*, etc.

CHAPTER ONE

THE LANGUAGE

I. The history of the language

1. The Vedic language

Sanskrit belongs to the Indian branch of the great family of the Indo-European languages. 'Indo-Aryan' is the name given to all the speeches of Indo-European origin that are known to have existed on the territory of India through its history. Three periods are distinguished: First, an 'Old Indo-Aryan' which is the language of the Vedas and which classical Sanskrit has kept alive down to the present day. Second, a 'Middle Indo-Aryan', or 'Middle Indian' for short, which groups together all the languages derived from the old form and which are attested since the centuries immediately preceding the Christian era until about the tenth century by literature and other documents (the Pāli of the Buddhist scriptures, the Ardhamāgadhī of the Jaina scriptures, and the Prākrits —literary as well as those of the inscriptions). Lastly a 'New Indo-Aryan' (NIA) which groups together the various languages which, from these manifold roots, have become even more diversified all over the Indian subcontinent and are the great living languages of most of the present day States of India. 'Indo-Aryan' moreover is contrasted with 'Dravidian', the name given to the other great family of languages of the subcontinent and represented mainly by Tamil, Kannaḍa, Telugu, etc. of the southern states of the peninsula. The most common idea, and the most frequently accepted one since the nineteenth century, is that Dravidian is a group of languages indigenous to India and that Indo-Aryan came from outside. But there is no Indian document that provides evidence that during the course of history, even in the most distant past, users of Indo-Aryan speeches had ever been aware of any foreign origin of their language.

The designation 'Vedic language' for the Old Indo-Aryan is based on the fact that the documents through which we know it comprise the corpus of texts called by the generic name of Veda. Indian tradition classifies these texts into several strata: four *Saṃhitās* or verse collections of religious hymns (*Ṛgveda*), of songs (*Sāmaveda*), of liturgical formulas (*Yajurveda*, partly in prose), of prayers for various purposes (*Atharvaveda*); *Brāhmaṇas* or commentaries on the preceding texts in prose; *Āraṇyakas* and *Upaniṣads*, or more speculative commentaries in prose; *Sūtras* or technical manuals relating to the rituals, customs, etc. Tradition also recognises, in theory, a very large number of schools, 21 for the *Ṛgveda*, 100 for the *Yajurveda*, 1000 for the *Sāmaveda*, 9 for the *Atharvaveda*. A school is defined by a recension of a *Saṃhitā* and a chain of texts that depend on it, or in other words a *Brāhmaṇa*, an *Āraṇyaka*, an *Upaniṣad* and a *Sūtra*. The two classifications therefore overlap. In the minds of well-read Indians all these works belong to a single period and to a single geographical region.

of 'so many times'. On the other hand, a treaty between the Hittite king Suppiluliuma and the Mitannian king Mattiwaza contains a list of gods invoked by the signatories. At the end of the list of the gods of the Mitannian side appear the names: *Mitra Uruwana Indar Nasattiyana*. They are the names of well-known Vedic gods: Mitra, Varuṇa, Indra, the twins Nāsatya. The first two are followed by the Hurrian suffix *śil* which means 'two of them'. We see here a literal Hurrian translation of the Vedic compound *mitrā́-váruṇā* in which the dual ending and the accent are retained for both members.

Historical documents reveal no explanation for the presence in Mitanni of specialists in chariot-borne warfare acquainted with the Vedic language and religion. But an important point is to be remembered by the historian of languages. We have here a dated use of a sample of the Vedic language. But this material is too sparse to be put into a relation with specific texts and for working out their chronology. But it attests at least to the existence of the Vedic language in about the middle of the second millennium BC. As regards the end of the formation of the Vedic corpus, this period is dated by the advent of Buddhism which seems to be acquainted with the later *Upaniṣads*. The Buddha, whose date is also disputed, is believed to have lived in the fifth century BC.

If this is so, Vedic would be a language whose output stretched across a millennium and over a vast area, that of the Indo-Gangetic plain. It cannot thus be envisaged as a single unit. We must determine on the one hand its dialectal variations, on the other its evolution during the course of time. There is yet another factor to be considered. What we know of it is only the literary productions of poets and experts in religious practice. We may wonder if the people or peoples as a whole used the same speech. It is likely that the Vedic of the texts diverged from popular dialects. We have no document on the latter. We shall see below how the well-read professionals preserved their texts and their scholarly language. We see here and now that the Vedic of the texts must have existed in the midst of popular dialects which must have influenced it.

To sum up, Vedic was in the beginning an old Indo-Aryan specialising in a well-defined form of religious poetry, and which developed over a millennium of time, and propagated itself over all the north of the Indian subcontinent, in the midst of various popular Indo-Aryan speeches that were evolving faster than itself.

These popular languages are documented for us only from the third century BC by the inscriptions of the emperor Aśoka. They are termed 'Middle Indo-Aryan'. They differ widely from one frontier to the other of his vast empire. It would be too simplistic to regard them as direct derivatives of Vedic. They are probably the result of the evolution of the old popular speeches contemporaneous with Vedic and from which it diverged through its specialised literary role and its resistance to natural evolution.

Vedic phonetics clearly stands apart from that of Avestan by a much greater preservation of the Indo-European sounds and by the absence of the Iranian innovations. For, it preserves the distinction between the voiceless and the voiced, between the aspirated and the non-aspirated, and practically ignores the spirantisation so common in Iran. The greatest innovation of Vedic is the adoption of retroflex stops, in opposition to the dentals. This phenomenon has been attributed to an influence of Dravidian which is strongly characterised by this contrast. But it has also been shown that the retroflexion had already begun in Indo-Iranian. An important feature of Vedic is the preservation of the accent. There exist as a rule three tones of musical character: a raised tone (*udātta*), a low tone (*anudātta*, literally 'unraised'), and a modulated or rising-falling tone (*svarita*) that enables the passing from the raised to the low. In a polysyllabic word there is a single raised tone, necessarily followed by a modulated tone, the other syllables being pronounced with a low tone. Incidentally, there can be a very low tone and a tone different from the others called atony for cases of pronunciation of an entire word with a single tone. Hence, there are five possible notes in total. The single raised tone constitutes the accent of the word, but it is one of pitch, not intensity. The place of the tone can differentiate two words that are otherwise identical in form, and is therefore significant: for example *bráhman* with a raised tone (transcribed here with the acute accent on the initial syllable) is neuter and refers to the incantation recited in the course of a ritual, to the effectual word of the priest, to the power of this word, of the sacrifice, etc., whereas *brahmán* with the tone on the final syllable is masculine and is the name of an officiating priest at the sacrifice. The tone has also considerable morphological and syntactical value. It marks the subordinate clause. In the sentence personal forms of the verb are not normally accented.

In the field of morphology, the most strikingly original Vedic features are some case endings, the use of the subjunctive and of an injunctive intermediate between the subjunctive and the indicative, and a surprising number of infinitive endings. There is a very great wealth of verb forms. The root *kṛ* 'to do' has some 160 distinct forms in Vedic (as against 30 in Avestan). There are as many as 16 infinitive forms. Moods and tenses are numerous and are distinguished by subtle nuances: there are three past tenses, etc. The subordinate clause formed mainly by using the relative pronoun is abundantly represented. There is above all a very great use of the particles which play an essential role in the sentence. The verbal prefix is a particle qualifying the meaning of the verbal root, but is not necessarily compounded with the verb, can be separated from it by several words, the order of the words being totally free as a rule.

2. Evolution and preservation of Vedic. The recitation of the Vedas

The earliest Vedic hymns testify already to a high degree of linguistic awareness of its authors. It appears for example in the play on the etymology of words. Thereafter, while the language seems to evolve relatively little, the knowledge of its structures develops considerably. Conservatism and linguistic awareness seem to go hand in hand. That could only have increased the distance between the 'popular' language of the non-specialists and the language of the experts in religion, since the former is always capable of a spontaneous evolution. In this situation it is important, for following the evolution of Vedic, to describe the preservationist measures which have influenced its destiny, to determine its environment that consisted of other forms of speech, to uncover the diverse and fluctuating influence of these forms of speech whose own evolution was probably much faster.

The first act of preservation is the organisation of the transmission of the Vedic texts, in the absence of writing. The Vedic texts began to be transmitted orally from master to disciple, by word of mouth, the quality of the transmission depending on human memory. The Veda, literally 'knowledge', called also '*śruti*' literally 'hearing' is seen as 'memory-matter' or 'auditory data', not as a book of Scripture. The recitation is the decisive factor of the preservation. Eleven methods of recitation have been codified during the course of the Ages. At least three are of great antiquity. The starting idea is that the same text can be presented in several forms. Each of these forms is learnt independently of the others. Once the reciter has memorised all the eleven, one after the other, he can then compare them and knowing the encoding rule for each see if there is indeed agreement between all, detect an occasional lapse of memory or an alteration when there appears a deviation in a recitation, and correct this fault. In this way will be preserved the integrity of the text. There are three basic forms and eight derivatives.

The first encoding consists in reciting each stanza continuously (*Saṃhitā*) without a pause between words, except for the mid-stanza pause. This is the most natural situation, reproducing that of the ordinary language in which the sentence is the most compact string possible. In Vedic that implies the application of phonetic changes at the point where the words are joined to each other. The final syllable of almost every word undergoes two different phonetic treatments depending on whether it is followed by a pause or by another word. A final vowel contracts when followed by an initial vowel of the same sound, such and such final consonant assimilates such and such initial consonant of the following word, etc.

The second encoding consists in reciting the same text with a pause after each word (*pada*). That results in modification of the final syllable in a number of cases. That is also a great help for the correct understanding of the text. There are at times ambiguities because of several possibilities of dividing the same string of words. For the preservation of the meaning of the text the analysis into words has to be known. For example there is a string *súṣṭutaítu* which can be analysed into *sú-stutā etu* 'may [the goddess Speech], meetly lauded, go away' or into *sú-stutā ā́ etu* 'may she, meetly lauded, come [to us]' which is evidently the meaning intended. The meaning of 'to come' is obtained thanks to the verbal prefix *ā* qualifying the imperative of the verb *i* 'to go'. The verbal prefix disappears in the contractions determined by the continuous recitation. We also understand from such an example the importance that this analysis into words must assume in the eyes of the officiant who counts on the prayer for the successful accomplishment of his ritual, who believes in the effectiveness of this word, who knows that this effectiveness depends on the accuracy of his pronunciation and his comprehension. The fragility of word frontiers in Vedic, the fact that this language does not accord the same treatment to the frontiers of words and to those of morphemes (i.e. between noun or verb stem and suffix beginning with a vowel), and the fact that the demarcation between these two areas is not simple make the task of division of the continuous string into its constituent words very delicate. It is said to have been accomplished by the grammarian Śākalya whose date is not known to us, but of whom it can be said that he was earlier to Pāṇini and that, in the history of linguistics, his is the earliest existing work of a linguist. By separating the words of the *Ṛgveda,* Śākalya truly accomplished the work of a linguist. His analysis demonstrates an extensive knowledge of phonetics and morphology.

A third encoding consists in linking each word in the text to the following word, and giving a pause after each pair so formed. That results in the application to the final syllable of each word two phonetic treatments successively: before a pause and before the initial syllable of the next word. In the case cited above where a monovocalic word disappears in a contraction of vowels in a string, this recitation isolates it in a group of three words. The fixing of this recitation called 'by steps' (*krama-pāṭha*) is due to a grammarian of the name Bābhravya and is of equal antiquity. With the use of the particle *iti* as an indicator of pause and some other rules governing the case of compounds, etc. these three encodings provide much advanced information on the form of the text and of the elements that are useful for a proper understanding of it. They are thus considered as a foundation (*prakṛti*).

Eight other encodings (*aṣṭa-vikṛti*) are derived from the material furnished by the first three. They do not bring additional information, but can serve as cross-checks for the detection and correction of errors. Each comprises an arrangement rule for individual words and pairs of words. For example the *jaṭā-pāṭha* ('in plaits') recitation consists in enunciating the first pair, repeating it in reverse order, reciting it in the normal order and giving a pause: ab ba ab | ; the *ghana-pāṭha* ('dense') recitation takes the first pair, reverses it, takes the group of the first three words, reverses it, repeats it in the given order, gives a pause: ab ba abc cba abc | , etc.

Given the verse VIII.100.11 of *Ṛgveda* in *saṃhitā*:

Devī́ṃ vā́cam ajanayanta devā́s tā́ṃ viśvárūpāḥ paśávo vadanti |
Sā́ no mandréṣam ū́rjaṃ dúhānā dhenúr vā́g asmā́n úpa súṣṭutaítu ||

'The deities generated Goddess Speech, and beings of every figure speak her. May she, the Gladdener, yielding food and vigour, the Milch-cow Speech, approach us, meetly lauded',
we obtain:

Pada: devī́m | vā́cam | ajanayanta | devā́ḥ | tā́m | viśvárūpāḥ | paśávaḥ | vadanti |
Sā́ | naḥ | mandrā́ | íṣam | ū́rjam | dúhānā | dhenúḥ | vā́k | asmā́n | úpa | sú-stutā | ā́ | etu ||

Krama: devī́ṃ vā́cam | vā́cam ajanayanta | ajanayanta devā́ḥ | devā́s tā́m | tā́m viśvárūpāḥ | viśvárūpāḥ paśávaḥ | viśvárūpā iti viśvá-rūpāḥ | paśávo vadanti | vadantīti vadanti | ... úpa súṣṭutā | súṣṭutaítu (group of three words) | súṣṭutéti sú-stutā | aítu | etv ity etu |

Jaṭā: devī́ṃ vā́caṃ vā́caṃ devī́ṃ devī́ṃ vā́cam | vā́cam ajanayantājanayanta vā́caṃ vā́cam ajanayanta | ajanayanta devā́ devā́ ajanayantājanayanta devā́ḥ | devā́s tā́ṃ tā́ṃ devā́ devā́s tā́ṃ | tā́ṃ viśvárūpā viśvárūpās tā́ṃ tā́ṃ viśvárūpāḥ | viśvárūpāḥ paśávaḥ paśávo viśvárūpā viśvárūpāḥ paśávaḥ | viśvárūpāḥ iti viśvá-rūpāḥ | paśávo vadanti vadanti paśávaḥ paśávo vadanti | vadantī́ti vadanti | ... úpa súṣṭutā súṣṭutā súṣṭutópópa súṣṭutā | súṣṭutāítv etv ā́ súṣṭutā súṣṭutāítu (groups of three words) | súṣṭutéti sú-stutā | aítu | etv ity etu |

Ghana: devī́ṃ vā́caṃ vā́caṃ devī́ṃ devī́ṃ vā́cam ajanayantā-janayanta vā́caṃ devī́ṃ devī́ṃ vā́cam ajanayanta | vā́cam ajanayantā-janayanta vā́caṃ vā́cam ajanayanta devā́ devā́ ajanayanta vā́caṃ vācam ajanayanta devāḥ | ...

The text of the *Ṛgveda* alone consists of 10462 verses and 153826 words. The learning, by hearing alone, of just the continuous recitation (*saṃhitā*) takes two years, that of the eleven some twelve years. The child is initiated into it at the tender age of six to eight years, when his memory has the maximum capability of being fed with material. Thereafter the recitation becomes a profession. The first duty of a reciter is to teach it, since that will ensure the transmission. Moreover, a religious value is attached to it. It is a ritual performed in homes and temples, on certain occasions, for various purposes the nature of which has varied from one region to another during the course of history. This ritual is most often financed by a devotee. It is a ritual that is still alive at the present time and the profession is still practised. Whereas the early antiquity of the first three recitations is certain, it is probable that the eight others are not as old. We do not know when they originated. What is undoubtedly true is the success of the oral transmission of the Vedic texts across more than four millennia, even before the appearance of writing, which is not very old in India. We observe that at the present time when the aid of writing is available there are still reciters who can completely do without it. To our knowledge, only the first two recitations, continuous and word by word, have been written down in the past and printed in the 19th century (*editio princeps* of the *Ṛgveda* by Max Müller). The other recitations have never been committed to writing, apart from small samples (cf. appendix of the recent edition of Satvalekar). A program to have them written by a computer was made for the first time in 1991. These recitations are practised most commonly for the *Ṛgveda* and the *Taittirīya-Saṃhitā* of the *Yajurveda*. There are also reciters of the *Śukla-Yajurveda* (white *Yajurveda*) and the *Atharvaveda*, but far fewer in number. The *Sāmaveda* is not recited by these methods, but is chanted. Both the text and the melody are memorised by hearing. There are also several methods of singing, and it takes a logn time to learn all of them. This tradition is still alive in several regions of India (Tamil Nadu, Kerala, etc.). It is probably the only case in the world of transmission of music from very early antiquity. Some regional modifications may have taken place during the course of history. But we have sound reasons to believe that the proportion of innovation is less than that of preservation.

3. Pāṇini, Kātyāyana, Patañjali

After the codification of the recitation for the preservation and the ritual use of texts, we see the emergence of a remarkable codification of the use of the language. Its stated goal is preservation, ease of learning, and correct interpretation or comprehension. This codification is divided into four disciplines of the study of speech: phonetics (*śikṣā*), grammar (*vyākaraṇa*), vocabulary (*nighaṇṭu*), metre (*chandas*). With the study of astronomy (*jyotiṣa*) and that of ceremonial (*kalpa*) they are said to constitute the six ancillaries of the Veda, called *Vedānga*. The most important of these ancillaries is grammar. The most remarkable is that of Pāṇini, whose date is disputed, but who may safely be situated within a period of 2 or 3 centuries centred on 500 BC.

Pāṇini has composed a list of formulae called *sūtra* (the name also applies to each individual formula) serving to form words and sentences from a given material of minimal elements. It is entitled *Vyākaraṇa-sūtra* 'Formulae for [the] construction [of words]', or *Aṣṭādhyāyī*, 'the eight lessons', because it is divided into eight parts, each being subdivided into four quarters. It comprises both lists of primary elements, and a programme for the combination of these elements. These elements are the phonemes, the roots, groups of words sharing a grammatical feature, morphemes (suffixes) having a meaning and which are placed necessarily after roots or noun stems, augments devoid of meaning which play a phonetic or morphological role, and various phonetic substitutes. The programme is made up of operating rules as well as conventions necessary for the application of the rules. It is composed in a true metalanguage very apt to its purpose, achieving the maximum brevity, which makes it easy to memorise, and is the first and foremost example of the formalisation of a technical exposition in the universal history of sciences. Because of its practical objective and form, it cannot be compared with a systematic grammar of a European type. By contrast, its resemblance to a modern computer program is striking. Its value can be judged from its performance: for 2500 years it has been the most used practical manual of Sanskrit. In the course of history other manuals have been compiled. Nine schools of grammar have been established. Some have enjoyed a definite success, but none equalled that which was established by Pāṇini. In any case they differ very little from the Paninian model.

Pāṇini does not give a name to the language whose structure is being described by him. He uses two terms: *bhāṣā* 'spoken language' and *chandas* '[text in] verse'. What he describes is therefore the language that he spoke. But his learning was supplemented by Vedic texts which he must have memorised, perhaps, to be precise, the *Yajurveda* of the Kaṭha school. Now, he had observed in these texts a certain number of differences from his everyday use. He accounts for what historians of language call 'archaisms', by accommodating them in specific rules. He takes a non-historical, rather structuralist, view of his language. He has received the spoken language from his parents and the Vedic texts from his master. This constitutes his learning. His grammatical formulae show how he uses his knowledge in practice and they are thus an invaluable document on the cultural awareness of an educated Indian of antiquity.

Through this document Pāṇini appears to us as being a follower of the Vedic religion, possessing a great literary knowledge, gifted with an undisputed scientific genius and coming to possess in this way an acute linguistic awareness. He belongs to a period that is perhaps a millennium later to that of the poets of the *Ṛgveda*. The examination of his work can give us an idea of the extent and the modes of evolution of the Vedic language. It can be said that for such a long interval of time the changes are minimal. The phonetics remains the same, one notices just the disappearance of the semi-vowel retroflex *ḷ* which is replaced by the voiced occlusive *ḍ*. The *saṃdhi* is more systematised, but does not innovate. In morphology there is abandonment of doublets, i.e. variant forms of morphemes, infinitive suffixes, terminations, etc., or in other words all that is unnecessary. The wealth of verb forms becomes reduced. The most important loss is that of the subjunctive and the injunctive. On the other hand there is a substantial enrichment of derivation and especially composition. The major innovation is the growth in the stock of basic elements, i.e., roots and morphemes. In the last analysis, we see that in the knowledge of Pāṇini Vedic still exists, in practice, in the midst of new material. An impressive survival is that of tone. Pāṇini spoke a language that still included the tones of the most ancient Vedic. He describes the facts of tonality not only for the Vedic forms, but also for all other forms of his spoken language. We know that the tone was to be discarded later. Likewise he also knows the nuances in meaning which differentiate the various past tenses, future tenses, etc. in Vedic (the use of the perfect for past events to which the speaker had not been a witness, the use of the imperfect for the past which is not of today, etc.), nuances which were to fall into disuse later. He considers that the verbal prefix normally joins with the verb, while recognising the Vedic tmesis. He thus represents a transitional period between Vedic and classical Sanskrit.

It has often been said that his language was artificial. Some have doubted its reality and have denied it the status of a living language. Recall that the linguistic awareness in an individual implies a certain systematisation and this is especially true in the case of Pāṇini who has had a very advanced concern for codification. Nevertheless it cannot be denied that Pāṇini spoke the language that he has described. He teaches a number of idiomatic uses. Alongside the rules serving to create new uses, there are a number of completed forms presented as they are (*nipātana*), forms which resist analysis, exceptions to the general rules, fossilised forms, unique items which cannot serve as models for new formations. This part of his *Aṣṭādhyāyī* lets us have a glimpse of a particularly living aspect of his language. For the idioms are attestations of living usage, not the creations of grammarians.

It is fairly difficult to determine the location in which Pāṇini's Sanskrit was used. According to a tradition that only dates from a millennium after his time, he lived at Śalātura (north of Attock, in today's Pakistan). But we also see that Pāṇini mentions minute dialectal details of the region of Punjab: a tank, he says, is called by its founder's name, with a suffix *a* and an initial tone north of Vipāś (modern Bias), with the same suffix but with a final tone south of this river. The fact that he had such good knowledge of minor dialectal variations makes one think that he belonged to this region. On the other hand he mentions some grammatical facts peculiar to regions equally distant from this centre, from Kashmir down to the eastern part of the Gangetic basin. And to read his description it does seem that his language was being spoken over this vast territory of the Indo-Gangetic plain, nearly in the whole of it. Now, as we have seen, we have every reason to think that it was not the only language spoken over this territory. Even though we do not have documentary evidence for this from Pāṇini's period, we know that popular Indo-Aryan languages were in use in his time and even much before. Those which are known to us by the inscriptions of Aśoka (third century BC) are not derived from the language of Pāṇini, but from the oldest forms of Old Indo-Aryan. Pāṇini's language coexisted with some of these, which influenced it. For example, in old Vedic a root *nṛt* 'to dance' is attested in some verb forms and a primary derivative *nṛti*. A feature of Middle Indian is that it does not preserve the vowel *ṛ* and substitutes it with an *a*; it accentuates also the Indian phenomenon of retroflexion of the dentals. The stem *nṛt* had naturally to change into the form *naṭ*; it is found later in the Pāli *naṭa* 'dancer', in Prakrit further changed with extension of the retroflexion and voicing, *ṇaḍa*, etc. Now, Pāṇini in his list of roots gives *nṛt* with the meaning of 'to dance' and two roots *naṭ*, one meaning 'to dance', the other 'to tremble'. In *naṭ* 'to dance' we recognise the form of Middle Indian derived from the old *nṛt*. On the other hand there is in Dravidian a root **naḍu* 'to tremble' attested in extensions such as the Tamil *naṭuṅku* 'to tremble', *naṭalai* 'trembling', the Kannaḍa *naḍugu* 'to tremble', *naḍa* 'while trembling', etc. in the old texts (*Cilappadikāram* in old Tamil, *Paṃpa-bhārata* in old Kannaḍa, etc.). Pāṇini's language probably made a double borrowing, that of *naṭ* 'to dance' from Middle Indian and that of *naṭ* 'to tremble' from Dravidian. And it did more than borrow a word. It extracts roots from the foreign usages and treats them as its own roots, adjoining to them its suffixes, its morphophonemic rules, etc., applying to them suffixes and conjugation, as it does for the root *nṛt* which it inherited from Vedic. Middle Indian and Dravidian are found sanskritised in this way. Pāṇini's language is, then, the sum of a Vedic heritage and a transposition of Middle Indian into this mould.

In this way Vedic perpetuated itself, preserving its structure, losing relatively little of its material, and coexisting with Middle Indian, not to say Dravidian, by assimilating them. This situation which we observe in Pāṇini is that of Sanskrit in every age. The coexistence of a multiplicity of languages is a remarkable fact of the linguistic history of India. The study of the society reveals in the same way the coexistence of several social strata. Pāṇini represents a class of scholarly experts of religion. His language is more the language of his class than the language of a region. And if his language spread over a vast territory, it is probably because the class to which he belonged had considerably extended its influence, its religion and its profession. This class lived in symbiosis with the other classes of society everywhere where the Vedic religion was accepted. At the same time, the language that it used adapted itself wherever it was used, without changing its structures, but by assimilating new material. It was perhaps not very much used by the other classes, but was certainly understood. As regards its speakers, whom we can visualise from the example of Pāṇini, they probably knew the vulgar dialects, understood them, but did not use them. Sanskrit must be considered as their first living language.

After Pāṇini we follow the linguistic history of India increasingly easily, because an abundance of various documents have come down to us. Regarding Sanskrit we have the works of two later grammarians who continued the work of their predecessor. Kātyāyana made a supplement to the *Vyākaraṇa-sūtra*, called *Vyākaraṇa-vārttika*. *Vārttika* is the name given to a formula which critically examines, corrects and supplements a *sūtra*, or else spells out its extent and modes of application. Next Patañjali made a commentary on the *sūtras* and their supplement, entitled *Vyākaraṇa-bhāṣya*. The *bhāṣya* is a 'discourse' on a *sūtra* and the *vārttikas* relating to it, very often taking the form of a dialogue between several masters who examine the formulas, discuss their performance in the formation of words and sentences, suggest new interpretations that can open up new fields of application, and occasionally decide on the needlessness of some of the teachings and their supplements. This commentary is often called *Vyākaraṇa-mahā bhāṣya*, literally 'the great commentary on the formation [of words]'. The qualification 'great' conveys the imposing volume of the work as well as its high intellectual quality. It is a high point in the history of Indian thought.

What is most innovative in Kātyāyana and especially in Patañjali in comparison with Pāṇini is their art of text interpretation. Starting from a very keen awareness of the natural procedures of comprehension of language, they used these procedures rationally as tools for creation of meaning from a text. Pāṇini had made a formalisation of expression by language by using and exploiting to the best the natural possibilities of expression. His successors made a formalisation of the comprehension of language. An example of their process of interpretation is that which can be deduced from an apparent superfluity of a statement. They start from the natural principle of the absence of redundancy in an expression. The author of a sentence has first the desire for expressing an idea. For each element of his idea he uses a meaningful form, and only one such form, that corresponds to it. The possibility of appearance of a form materialises due to a desire on the part of the speaker to express a meaning. Once the meaning is expressed, there is no longer any chance of the appearance of a corresponding form. Hence there exists no redundancy of expressive element in speech. This principle may be considered as having been applied to its fullest extent by the author of the *sūtras*, formulae characterised by rigour and brevity. If the interpreter encounters in a statement a form which he can prove to be superfluous, he must either conclude from it that the form of the statement is invalid or pursue his effort of comprehension until he has found the information that can legitimately be inferred from the statement that has been called into question. Patañjali's attitude to the *sūtras* of Pāṇini is the tireless pursuit of the effort of comprehension. He lays down the principle that Pāṇini's teaching is perfect and that it is for him to understand it.

Let us take an example of Patañjali's interpretation. Sanskrit has a periphrastic perfect in which an invariant form in *-ām* is followed by a personal form of perfect of an auxiliary verb: *īhāṃ cakre* 'he endeavoured' (root *īh*, morpheme *ām*, root *kṛ* with reduplication which adds *ca,* and ending *e* of third person singular of the perfect). Pāṇini constructs this form in the following way. The speaker wishes to express the meaning of the agent of the action of endeavouring in the past; a rule produces in relation with these meanings the root *īh* and a suffix with the theoretical form *liṭ*; another rule prescribes the morpheme *ām* after this root: *īh-ām-liṭ*; another elides *liṭ*; another then prescribes after the form in *ām* a joint use of the root *kṛ* 'to do' followed by the suffix *liṭ*, which determines for *kṛ* the application of a series of rules of reduplication and for *liṭ* a substitution with the termination *e*. The statement of the rule for the joint use of *kṛ* is: *kṛñ cānuprayujyate liṭi* 'and *kṛñ* is used jointly when there is *liṭ*' (3.1.40). Patañjali remarks then that the form terminating with *ām* does not have a sufficiently clear meaning by itself, *īhām* is an invariant, and a personal verb is lacking. Now, it is the speaker who, in order to convey the meaning which he wishes to express, calls up the root and the morpheme. The rules do not take the place of the speaker's will. Therefore the cause of the appearance of the joint use of the auxiliary verb is the speaker's will. There is no need for a rule to prescribe the use of the auxiliary. Patañjali then concludes that one must understand another reading implicit in this statement, superfluous otherwise. *Kṛ*$^{\tilde{n}}$ is not to be understood as being the simple enunciation of *kṛ*, but the abbreviated enunciation of three roots, *kṛ* 'to do', *bhū* 'to be' and *as* 'to be'. And he shows that this interpretation is in conformity with the abbreviation procedures of Pāṇini's metalanguage. Lest it should be said that even this teaching was needless, because it is natural for the speaker to choose as auxiliary a verb having one of these general meanings, Patañjali then asserts that one must understand here a teaching on the position of the auxiliary at the second place and without any possibility of interposition of any other word.

If we note that the newest information produced by this interpretation is the use of *bhū* and *as* as auxiliaries since, strictly speaking, the *sūtra* mentions only *kṛ*, then we discern the motivation for the effort of the interpreter. A fact determined by the historian of Indo-Aryan is the use of only the auxiliary *kṛ* in the ancient period, the use of *as* appearing at the end of the Vedic period, that of *bhū* being the last of all. It does seem that Pāṇini had known only the use of *kṛ*, or else he would not have resorted to a hidden statement whose comprehension can only be obtained by the roundabout means of interpretation. But in the time of Patañjali the uses of *as* and *bhū* must have become familiar. Patañjali wanted to read this fact in the Paninian statement. He adapted the practical manual to his times. He increased the effectiveness of this tool for the construction of words in such a way as to make it as effective for the language of his time as it was for that of Pāṇini.

We see that recourse to these interpretation procedures suggests that the language has been changing. All that is added by way of information to Pāṇini's text is not forgetfulness on his part, it is rather the inflow of new material into the language. From Pāṇini to Patañjali Sanskrit enriched itself even more considerably by borrowings assimilated with the inherited structure. Kātyāyana is placed in the period of Aśoka (middle of third century BC), Patañjali in the second century BC or, according to some, in the first century AD. Their language developed in the midst of various forms of Middle Indian which were emerging from the status of simple spoken dialects for everyday use to the status of official languages of organised states, as well as literary and religious languages. The period immediately preceding and following the Christian era is one in which India was trying to discover a common language for its civilisation. Sanskrit did not compel recognition at once. It has had as its rivals several forms of Middle Indian: the Prākrits which the various empires used in their edicts, Pāli in which the Buddhists were trying to fix the word of their founder and the Ardhamāgadhī which the Jainas used likewise for their religious canon. Sanskrit became established in the royal and other administrations only after the Christian era and never completely. It became imperative for the Buddhists only in a certain number of schools, notably the Mahāyāna branch, and for the Jainas only in their extra-canonical literature. It has nevertheless very largely overtaken its rivals, spreading over all of Asia, while the forms of Middle Indian remained regional, and Pāli and Ardhamāgadhī remained confined to the context of the religions in which they were born. One reason for its success is probably its very great adaptability to the borrowing and the assimilation of material from other languages.

4. The stabilisation of Sanskrit

It has often been said that Sanskrit was fixed during Pāṇini's time and a great responsibility for this phenomenon has been attributed to this grammarian. One often hears that with Pāṇini Sanskrit had become a dead language. In reality, what Pāṇini in fact did was to impart to the users of his language an awareness of its structures of formation. To speak without linguistic awareness is not the same thing as speaking while knowing consciously how one constructs one's speech. The possession of a well-defined linguistic awareness enables the speaker to control his acts of speech. It is not strictly speaking an artificial stabilisation of the language. For that a specific will is needed. Pāṇini, as we saw, had the will to preserve the Vedic heritage at the very most. He also let his language enrich itself with material from other languages. This attitude was already present amongst his predecessors. It would also be that of his successors. And the language still evolved between Pāṇini and Patañjali. As for the Sanskrit of Patañjali it was still a living language. Patañjali gave as norm and model of what he saw as the best language his well-read contemporaries. He called them *śiṣṭa* 'educated'. He described them as inhabiting Āryāvarta, the geographical name of the Indo-Gangetic plain. He defined them above all by their social standing, and within their group by their psychological qualities: 'those who are brahmans, who have a good stock of grains, who are without greed, who are disinterested and who have fully mastered some science without difficulty, those are the educated people worthy of respect'. To the objection that, if there were educated people who were an authority in the matter of language, Pāṇini's grammar was needless, Patañjali replied that it simply served to recognise who were the educated people : 'Someone who studies the *Aṣṭādhyāyī* sees another who does not study it and who uses the words that it prescribes. He observes: there is, truly, a divine grace or a natural gift in him who does not study the *Aṣṭādhyāyī*, and who uses the words that it prescribes. That person truly knows also the other correct words [which it does not prescribe]'. Patañjali considered then that a gifted person could learn language very well, naturally, without studying grammar, that there was a language that was innate and that grammar did not describe it in its totality. The Sanskrit of Patañjali was the living language of a class of his contemporaries. It was their first language, learnt because they were born in a good family of the proper region. One could then learn Sanskrit without the *Aṣṭādhyāyī* and one could enrich his knowledge of Sanskrit from another source.

It would not be always so. Sanskrit continued to evolve during the period close to the Christian era. It lost an important feature, the tone, still taught for the spoken language by Patañjali, and still pronounced by him (for the rules of tone he gave his examples by pronouncing the accented words). After him the tone would only subsist for the Vedic texts learnt by heart according to the very old methods of recitation. This loss is perhaps a sign of a change in the status of Sanskrit. It was the loss of a particularly living feature of the language and the sign of its transition to the state of second language, acquired by a specific education, and not the result of birth. For in the learning of a second language pronunciation is the most difficult thing to acquire to perfection, precisely because it is not easy to get rid of the features of pronunciation of one's first language; one often retains the accent of his mother tongue. This phenomenon can be observed in the Sanskrit of our day. We see Sanskrit pronounced differently in different provinces of India and coloured by the phonetics of the various modern languages, Indo-Aryan or Dravidian: the *a* becomes *o* in Bengal, the *s ś ṣ* are pronounced alike in Orissa, the contrast between voiceless and voiced, and between non-aspirated and aspirated, is blurred in Tamil Nadu, etc. That is not the result of ignorance of the Sanskrit phonetic system, but of the influence of the first language on the pandits who learn Sanskrit through theoretical grammar and master it as a second language. Such a serious alteration of the pronunciation resulting from the omission of tone by the well-educated who were aware of its existence and the rules for it by Pāṇini's grammar can only be explained by the influence of a first language that did not have a system of accentuation, and hence the transition of Sanskrit to the state of a second language. When did this change happen? There is no precise date for it, but the transformation must have taken place gradually during the early centuries of the Christian era. This change from the state of a language acquired spontaneously in the milieu in which one is born to that of second language learnt through grammar does not necessarily result in the decline of the language. It is perhaps responsible for a certain grammatical stabilisation. For grammar then becomes more than a set of rules to which one refers occasionally, it becomes an indispensable source. The tradition of the pandits perpetuated this stabilisation, in that it raised the teaching of the three grammarians to the level of norm and reference for the correct language, making a 'trinity of sages' (*munitraya*) of them, according the highest authority to the most recent when there was discord between them, in other words to Patañjali in the last resort.

On the other hand, this change leads the language into a preferred direction. For from the period when Sanskrit was being learnt mainly through the Paninian manual, it has become more dependent on the structures through which it had been described. We can show from an example that a grammar rule can influence the evolution of a language. Along with the rules describing the forms already attested, Pāṇini prescribes many other rules which also aim at new forms, which represent the capacity of the speaker to create them. By the side of the teaching of closed lists of already existing compounds, Pāṇini gives rules of composition which can account for the formation of compounds that have already been created in some past acts of speech, but leave the way open for the formation of new examples as yet unknown. Now, in the evolution of Indo-Aryan the compound is not a category that has developed abundantly. In contemporary living languages, it is not seen as a formation that is totally unfettered. The speaker feels a limit to its application, finds that the compound is improper beyond two or three words. Pāṇini has not formulated any limit of application for most of his composition rules. He did not rule out the compound of compounds, etc. From the time when his grammar became the major source of acquisition of the knowledge of Sanskrit, the rule of unlimited application was accepted as such. And we see a disproportionate development of composition, a feature peculiar to classical Sanskrit. There is no limit to the length of the compounds, no limit to the creation of new examples. The compound ends up by replacing the subordinate clause, in that it is an easy means of fitting word groups into one another.

In this way Sanskrit was constrained by its grammarians of old. It can be defined as a language whose structure is that which Pāṇini has described. Now there are structures which can be unconsciously present in the speaker and which the history of the language can at times bring to light. They illuminate the history of the formation of the language, but they do not describe the language such as its speakers know, because their awareness of Sanskrit is defined by the Paninian system. There are at times divergences between the structure revealed by history or by comparison with other Indo-European languages and the structure described by Pāṇini. For example, there is in Sanskrit an active past participle *kṛtavant* 'who has done' which Pāṇini constructs with a primary suffix *tavant* after the root *kṛ* 'to do', a form for which comparative grammar finds a parallel in the construction of the perfect with the auxiliary 'have' in many of the Indo-European languages of Europe, and comparative grammar analyses it into the root *kṛ*, primary suffix *ta* of passive past participle and secondary suffix *vant* expressing the idea of possession. There is, then, an old Indo-European formation using a morpheme meaning possession for transforming a passive past participle into active. Such a structure is unconsciously present in the speaker of Sanskrit who has learnt this language through Pāṇini's grammar. In his consciousness *kṛtavant* is a primary derivative, even though the word is historically formed as a secondary derivative.

We see how the Paninian linguistic awareness is an intimate part of the language. We must, then, define Sanskrit as a language of Indo-European origin, whose first known forms constitute the Vedic language, which during nearly two thousand years sees a first form of evolution in which it preserves its Vedic heritage and enriches itself with the influences of Middle Indian, and even Dravidian, tongues, is the subject of awareness of procedures of generation by Pāṇini, of procedures of comprehension by Patañjali, which is guided and fixed by this awareness that has become an integral part of itself, and will finally be learnt and used with this awareness during yet another nearly two millennia to the present day.

II. The structure of Sanskrit

To obtain a scientific presentation of Sanskrit it is important to describe it on the one hand from the point of view of its history which reveals features unconsciously present in the user and gives a number of elements of explanation, and on the other hand from the point of view of the trinity of grammarians, Pāṇini, Kātyāyana and Patañjali, because their description is an integral part of the language and the part of which the user is most conscious.

1. The name of Sanskrit

It is only around the 5th or the 6th century AD that we have reliable attestations to this word being used in reference to this language. We see that it has begun to be called by this name when it passed to the status of second language, learnt with the help of grammars, in other words when the procedures of formation and of comprehension codified from Pāṇini to Patañjali have become an integral part of it, have constituted the linguistic awareness of all of its users. The tradition of the pandits gives the word 'Sanskrit' (*saṃskṛta*) as meaning the form of speech 'constructed' by a grammar such as that of Pāṇini. The word is made with the suffix *ta* of passive past participle after the root *kṛ* 'to do' fitted with a verbal prefix *sam* bringing the idea of superior quality; a translation is often made by following the etymology: 'perfect'. But etymology is not adequate to render all the values of the term. The first meaning of *saṃskṛta* in everyday use, before the word was applied to speech, is 'made ready'. For an action to be accomplished it is necessary for various factors to come together. The term *saṃskāra* (action noun constructed from the same root) refers to all the preparations for an action, including the gathering together of the agent, the other factors, and the necessary material, this preparation having meaning only because of the goal, the accomplishment of something. What is *saṃskṛta* is what has been prepared in this way with an action in view. The word is used for example in reference to a cooked dish, because then it is ready for being eaten, to be digested and to nourish the human body. Cooking is a *saṃskāra* in that it makes substances capable of nourishing the body. *Saṃskāra* is then the gathering together of factors which confer on them ability. In this sense it is a bringing to perfection. This notion is applied in the field of social and religious life. The individual is prepared by rites called *saṃskāra* that make him fit for such and such activity, the initiation that makes him fit to study with a master, the marriage that renders him fit to live a period of life as a householder, etc. In the field of psychology *saṃskāra* is the organisation of the effects left in the unconscious by past experiences. This organisation makes the individual fit for new experiences. It is the acquisition of an organised knowledge that makes him fit to know and act. Language is a *saṃskāra*, in that it is a knowledge that makes the individual fit to accomplish new acts of speech.

Language is said to be *saṃskṛta* when it is prepared by grammar, in other words when it is accompanied by the awareness of its structures of formation and of comprehension codified by Pāṇini, etc. One can very well speak his mother tongue, acquired without grammatical education, and hence without a clear awareness of the structures. But to speak a language with an awareness of these two types of structures is another matter. We have already seen that language by this *saṃskāra* of grammar acquired an ability for preserving itself, as well as for enriching itself, by assimilating material from external sources. It is evident that it becomes more fit for intellectual activity also. It is a tool perfected for the functioning of the mind in every field of activity. This is how we can explain the fact that Sanskrit has become the vehicle of all the intellectual activities in which people have had the idea of engaging themselves in India during several millennia. We note moreover the extreme adaptability of Sanskrit to all the disciplines, its capacity for supplying new technical vocabularies, and for abbreviating itself by composition or secondary derivation, when the exercise of thought processes requires it e.g. in poetic creation or logical reasoning. The old Indo-Aryan is called Sanskrit precisely to account for this linguistic perfecting through linguistic awareness aimed at the optimal adaptation to intellectual activity.

2. The Paninian structures

Modern historical and comparative linguistics has inspired a description of Sanskrit through categories of words and sentences, with the usual classification of the European grammars into phonetics, morphology of the noun and the verb, and syntax. The best Sanskrit grammar of this type in the French language is that of Louis Renou (*Grammaire sanscrite*, Paris, Maisonneuve, 2nd edition, 1968). In English, the *Sanskrit Grammar* by W.D. Whitney (Harvard University Press, Cambridge, Massachusetts, several editions: 1879, 1889, 1931, etc., and a reprint by Motilal Banarsidass, Delhi, 1962) is noteworthy for the quality of its presentation and its great accuracy. The most exhaustive Sanskrit grammar is in German: *Altindische Grammatik* by Wackernagel. We shall briefly summarise only the Indian description of the Paninian school, less accessible in Europe, indicating, as we go, some parallels with the first.

The Ṣanskrit grammarians consider their language in terms of generation and comprehension.

A) The elements

a) The phoneme (*varṇa*) is the smallest element, having no meaning by itself but causing a string of sounds to change in meaning if it is changed. It is determined in an experimental manner by comparing similar words. For example, *k*, *y* and *s* are determined when we compare the words *kūpa* 'well' *yūpa* 'post', *sūpa* 'dish', because the sense changes when they are substituted for each other. The phonemes are 48 in number:

5 simple short vowels	*a*	*i*	*u*	*ṛ*	*ḷ*
4 simple long vowels	*ā*	*ī*	*ū*	*ṝ*	
4 diphthongs	*e*	*ai*	*o*	*au*	
2 ancillary sounds (nasalisation, voiceless aspirate)	*ṃ*	*ḥ*			

25 stops in 5 categories of 5 (in the order voiceless, voiceless aspirate, voiced, voiced aspirate, nasal)

velar	*k*	*kh*	*g*	*gh*	*ṅ*
palatals	*c*	*ch*	*j*	*jh*	*ñ*
retroflex	*ṭ*	*ṭh*	*ḍ*	*ḍh*	*ṇ*
dentals	*t*	*th*	*d*	*dh*	*n*
labials	*p*	*ph*	*b*	*bh*	*m*

4 semi-vowels	*y*	*r*	*l*	*v*
4 spirants	*ś*	*ṣ*	*s*	*h*

b)The root (*dhātu*) is a morpheme expressing the idea of activity in general with some series of particular successive acts leading to a result. Pāṇini gives a list of nearly 2,000 of them: *bhū* 'to be', *édha* 'to increase', etc.

c)The primary suffix (*kṛt-pratyaya*) is a morpheme which appears directly after a root and expresses one of the factors in the accomplishment of the action, the idea of an agent, etc. or the idea of the action itself. Most serve to form nouns. Others serve to create verb forms: these are affixes called *vikaraṇa* appearing after the roots and followed by personal endings; a series serves to form the stems of the present, etc. another those of the aorist, of the future, etc. Another group of *kṛt* serves to form verbal nouns followed by case endings, affixes with the sense of obligation, of participle, etc.

d)The secondary suffix (*taddhita-pratyaya*) is a morpheme added to a stem having already at least one suffix. Their meanings are very diverse. The same suffix has often several semantic values. There are suffixes of the same form, but distinguished by the tone, or the state of their stem.

e)The case endings: Seven endings (*sup-vibhakti*) express the relationship with the action signified by the root of the verb: idea of agent, etc. They are called by their order: first (nominative and vocative), second (accusative), third (instrumental), fourth (dative), fifth (ablative), sixth (genitive), seventh (locative). Each of them has 3 forms, singular, dual, plural.

f)The personal endings of the verb: 2 series of 9 endings (*tiṅ-vibhakti*), respectively *parasmaipada* endings employed when the benefit of the action goes to another (the active voice) and *ātmanepada* endings employed when the benefit of the action goes to the agent himself (the middle voice). This is true for roots which admit of both series. Many roots admit of only one of the series. These endings express a factor of the action, such as the idea of agent, or of object of the action, or the idea of action. In each series they express 3 numbers, singular, dual and plural and 3 persons: 1st person which is the 3rd of the European grammars, middle person (= the second person), last person (= the first person).

g)The feminine suffixes appear after *kṛt-* or *taddhita* derivatives and even compounds, and are followed by case endings.

h)The suffixes appearing at the end of compounds.

B) The generation of word types

a)The primary derivative (*kṛd-anta*) is formed by adding a *kṛt* suffix directly to a root. It is characterised by a tone depending on the suffix. Two suffixes of the same form and meaning can produce 2 derivatives differing by the accent: *tavya* produces *kartavyà* and *kartávya*. Two suffixes can be distinguished by the accent of their derivatives and by a nuance in meaning: *kti*^{c} produces a noun of action with a benedictive value and final tone *bhūtí* '(desired) welfare', *kti*^{n} produces a noun of action without any nuance and with an initial tone *gáti* 'motion'. The primary derivative is also characterised by the vocalic gradation of the root after which it appears. Every root can in effect take three vocalic forms: simple vowel (or zero grade), with *guṇa* substitute (technical term for *a, e, o*) (or normal grade), with *vṛddhi* substitute (technical term for *ā, ai, au*) (or strengthened grade), for example *ji-ta* 'vanquished', *je-tṛ* 'victor', *a-jai-ṣ-īt* 'vanquished', where the suffix ^{k}*ta* expressing the idea of object of the action, the suffix *tṛ* expressing the idea of agent, and the aorist suffix *sic* appear after the root *ji* 'to vanquish', etc.

b)The secondary derivative (*taddhita-anta*) is seen as the transformation of a phrase of inflected words, a transformation during the course of which a *taddhita* suffix is substituted for a word expressing its meaning and the internal inflectional ending is dropped. For example the phrase *gargasya apatyam* 'descendant of Garga' is transformed into *gārgya* in which *apatyam* is replaced by the suffix *ya*$^{\tilde{n}}$. The secondary derivative is characterised by a tone depending on the suffix and occasionally by a *vṛddhi* substitute of its first vowel. There is generally a choice between the phrase and the secondary derivative. It is a very productive category.

c)The compound (*samāsa*) is the transformation of a phrase of inflected words into a unit in which the case endings have been dropped. It is characterised by a single tone. There are many types of compound according to the nature of the starting phrase: determinative compound (*tatpurusa*), ex. *rājñaḥ puruṣaḥ* > *rājapuruṣaḥ* 'servant of the king'; possessive compound (*bahuvrīhi*), ex. *Bahavo vrīhayaḥ yasya* > *bahuvrīhiḥ* 'whose rice is plentiful'; copulative compound (*dvandva*) ex. *Dharmaś ca arthaś ca kāmaś ca mokṣaś ca* > *dharma-artha-kāma-mokṣāḥ* 'virtue, wealth, enjoyment and liberation [which are the 4 goals of man]', etc. In general there is a choice between the phrase and the compound.

C) The generation of the sentence

The speaker constructs his sentence out of a desire for expressing a meaning (*vivakṣā*). The most common procedure in the Paninian school makes the speaker start from the expression of the action. The wish to express an action situated in a past, present or future time summons a root. Then the desire to express the idea of agent or of object of the action produces one among the ten theoretical suffixes, such as l^{at} for the present, l^{it} for the past, etc. The desire to express a person, and a number, calls up a personal ending as substitute of *l*. The appearance of l^{at}, etc. determines the application of a rule for affixing a *vikaraṇa* between the root and itself, and possibly other morphophonemic or phonetic rules. At this stage the meaning already expressed is that of an action qualified by an agent; it is the meaning of the verb. If the speaker desires next to express the identity of the agent, that determines the appearance of a noun stem naming the individual playing this role. The idea of agent being already expressed in the verb, there is no new morpheme appearing for that. There is only the appearance of the first case ending which indicates that there is no meaning to be added to that of the stem. Next when the speaker desires to name the object of the action, that determines the appearance of the noun stem identifying this object. Next he will want to express the idea of object of the action. Since this idea is not yet expressed, the second case ending appears for that after the name of the object. Other noun stems will appear for indicating the different factors of the action which the speaker will want to mention. There are 6 factors of action (*kāraka*) that can be expressed by suffixes and case endings: agent (*kartṛ*) or locus of the action, object (*karman*) or locus of the result of the action, instrument (*karaṇa*), addressee or beneficiary (*saṃpradāna*), origin (*apādāna*), location (*adhikaraṇa*).

The speaker can also desire to express qualifications of one or the other of the terms employed. The qualifier (*viśeṣaṇa*) is seen as a factor of differentiation of the qualified within the category to which it belongs. For example the word *lotus* is given to a great variety of flowers; the word *blue* is a qualifier of the lotus in that it distinguishes the flower of this colour from the flowers of other colours. The relationship between the qualifier and the qualified is described as being their commonality of reference (*sāmānyādhikaraṇya*). This notion signifies that the two terms *lotus* and *blue* refer to the same object and describe it from different points of view: *lotus* refers to a flower by describing it by its species, *blue* refers to the same by describing it by its colour. The qualifier is seen as a name in the same way as the qualified. The commonality of reference entails agreement in case, gender and number.

Example of formation: *devadattaḥ agninā pacati odanam sthālyām* 'Devadatta by means of the fire cooks the rice in a pot':

Semantic data	morpheme	Paninian rule	result
Idea of action	root	bhūvādayo dhātavaḥ 1.3.1	
Sense of 'to cook'	*pac*	ḍupacàṣ pāke 1.718	pac
Idea of agent	lakāra	laḥ karmaṇi ca... 3.4.69	pac l
Present	$\text{l}^{\text{aṭ}}$	vartamāne laṭ 3.2.123	pac l
		lasya, tiptasjhi-... 3.4.77-78	
singular, 1st per.	ti^{p}	tiṅas trīṇi... 1.4.101 3.2.123	pac ti
	$^{\text{ś'}}\text{a}^{\text{p}}$-	kartari śap 3.1.68	pacati
identity of the agent	devadatta	prātipadikārtha... 2.3.46	devadattaḥ
identity of the object	odana		odana
idea of object	am	karmaṇi... 2.3.2	odana am
		ami pūrvaḥ 6.1.107	odanam
ident of the instr.	agni		agni
idea of instrument	$^{\text{ṭ}}\text{ā}$	kartṛkaraṇayos... 2.3.18	agni ā
	nā	ā ṅo... 7.3.120	agninā
identity of the place	sthālī		sthāli
idea of location	$^{\text{ṅ}}\text{i}$	saptamy... 2.3.36	sthālī i
	ām	ṅer ām... 7.3.116	sthālī ām
		iko yaṇ aci 6.1.77	sthālyām

D) The Comprehension

Comprehension involves an analysis which is simply the reverse of the formation procedure. It is based on 3 constitutive factors of the sentence, which make it a meaningful unit: mutual proximity (*saṃnidhi*) of the meaningful components, their fitness (*yogyatā*) to be constructed with one other, their semantic expectancy (*ākāṅkṣā*). Proximity leads to construction of words between them. Their fitness to bind themselves to each other gives an indication as regards the construction: for example a verb is apt to be constructed with a direct object complement only if it is transitive. On the other hand a word is not enough by itself generally, but has need to be constructed with another well-defined type of word. For example the transitive verb requires an object complement and other factors of action. This semantic expectancy is of two kinds: that which is already created by the nature of the word, like the need of an object for a transitive verb; that which is created by the desire of the speaker, when for example he adds a qualifier: in *candraḥ kumudabāndhavaḥ udeti* 'the moon, friend of the nocturnal lotuses, rises' the term *moon* is required by the need for an agent created by the verb *rises*, but the need for the qualifier *friend...* is created by the will of the author of the sentence.

A traditional method of analysis of the sentence in the Sanskrit schools presents this semantic expectancy of the various words with the help of questions each of which is a search for a significant component. Given the sentence:

vāg-arthāv iva saṃpṛktau vāg-artha-saṃpratipattaye |
jagataḥ pitarau vande pārvatī-parameśvarau ||

'To learn the word and the meaning, I salute the parents of the universe, the Daughter of the Mountain and the Supreme Lord who are united as the word and the meaning.' (Kālidāsa, *Raghuvaṃśa* I.1)

The analysis begins with the word: *vande* 'salute'. The root *vand* expresses the action of saluting. It needs to be completed by the following information:

-*kaḥ* 'who?' (question concerning the agent);
-*aham* 'I' (meaning conveyed by the ending *e* of the verb);

-*kau* 'whom?' (question relating to the object of the action);
-*pārvatī-parameśvarau* 'Pārvatī and Parameśvara';
-*kasmai* 'with a view to what?';
-*vāg-artha-pratipattaye* 'to learn the word and the meaning';
-*pārvatī-parameśvarau kathaṃbhūtau* 'Pārvatī and Parameśvara are how?';
-*pitarau* 'parents';
-*kasya* 'whose';
-*jagataḥ* 'of the universe';
-*punaḥ kathaṃbhūtau* 'again how are they?';
-*saṃpṛktau* 'united';
-*kāv iva* 'like what?';
-*vāg-arthāv iva* 'like the word and the meaning'.

Next the analyses of words are to be made. A secondary derivative like *pārvatī* is analysed by going back to the original group of words from which it was formed: *parvatasya apatyam strī* 'female descendant of the Mountain' (here it is the Himālaya, the father of Śiva's spouse). Similarly a compound is analysed by going back to the word group from which it was formed: *paramaś cāsāv īśvaraś ca* 'he who is supreme and lord' (common designation of the great god Śiva), etc.

In the school of the Paninian grammarians the knowledge produced by the sentence whose components are understood and analysed in this way is described schematically by a formulation such as: 'action of saluting (the meaning of *vand*), qualified by an agent who is me (meaning of the ending *e*), by an object (meaning of the accusative dual ending *au*) who is the Daughter of the Mountain and the Supreme Lord (meaning of the noun stem *pārvatī-parameśvara*), who are qualified (relationship indicated by the agreement of the ending *au* with that of the preceding word) by the property of being the object (meaning of the suffix *ta*) of the action of uniting (meaning of the root *saṃ-pṛc*), etc.

A number of approaches to sentence and word analysis have been elaborated in the Sanskrit schools in the course of time. They are on two general lines: the presentation morpheme by morpheme by separate propositions, and the continuous presentation as a long compound.

The procedures of comprehension are not restricted to this literal analysis of the morphemes on the basis of the morphemes. Other factors, such as context, criteria for the determination of meaning in cases of ambiguity, inferential procedures of the type similar to those described above regarding Patañjali, etc. enter into consideration and constitute the matter of the commentaries. At yet another level, that of the commentary on texts that are concerned with rituals, where the prescriptive sentence of a ritual for obtaining a material or spiritual result is analysed in this perspective, interpretation rules have been codified. This constitutes a discipline in its own right, distinct from and supplementary to grammar, called *Mīmāṃsā*. The fact that every Sanskrit man of letters, or *pandit,* is formed not only in the knowledge and the handling of the language, but also in these disciplines of analysis and exegesis, explains the extraordinary development, in quantity and refinement, of the exegetic literature in India.

3. The script

Sanskrit had to wait perhaps a number of centuries before being written. Script is attested in India by pictograms inscribed on seals in the Indus valley in the third millennium BC, forgotten and as yet undeciphered by modern science. Following that, it is attested by two scripts, *kharoṣṭhī* in the north-west of the country and *brāhmī* in the rest of the subcontinent, from the time of Aśoka in the third century BC. The first was only used for Middle Indian languages during a few centuries. The second has had a more considerable development, in that it has been used for a long time for writing several languages, has evolved by diversifying itself and can be considered as the mother of all the scripts in use in India down to the present day, as well as of a number of scripts of central and south-east Asia. The Sanskrit language, having been used in every period and in all regions, has been written in *brāhmī* and in all its derivatives wherever they were current.

The first written Sanskrit documents are inscriptions dating from the early centuries of the Christian era and fragments of manuscripts of Buddhist dramas on palm leaves found in central Asia and datable to the third or fourth century AD. Considering the antiquity of the Vedic literature, the relatively late appearance of written documents, the absence of direct mention of writing in the texts themselves before precisely the period of these first documents (the first certified mention of writing is found in Kātyāyana, with the word *lipi* of non-Indian origin, and with reference to a *yavanānī* 'greek' (?) writing. IV.1.49), and the minor role of writing in teaching in the ancient period, lead to the conclusion that all that has reached us of old Vedic and Sanskrit literature has been transmitted orally through memorisation alone over the course of centuries. This fact is confirmed by the example, still observable today, of the memorisation of the Vedas through the methods of recitation described above. Scripts only became a common tool for writing down Sanskrit and its vast literature after the Christian era, and the massive and regular production of manuscripts is a phenomenon of the Middle Ages.

The Sanskrit writings, as well as those of other languages, are in the form of inscriptions on stone —mostly walls of monuments or specially prepared stelae— or on copper plates where charters, panegyrics of monarchs, celebrations of endowments, etc. were concerned; and in the form of manuscripts on palm-leaf (*borassus flabelliformis Linn.* and *corypha umbraculifera Linn.*) in all of India and south-east Asia, on the inner bark of birch in Kashmir, on liber (inner bark) of agallochum (Sanskrit: *agaru*) in Bengal and Assam, and finally on paper whose use becomes common in India in the eleventh century. The scribe incised the characters on palm leaves in the south of India, drew them with reed pen and ink in the north and did the same on the other media. Several million Indian manuscripts, most of which in Sanskrit, are presently preserved in India (and incidentally in Europe) in state libraries and private collections, and this fragile heritage deserves much more care than it has been receiving until now.

The scripts used for writing Sanskrit, encountered most frequently in manuscript collections are: *nāgarī* (a script still used for Hindī, Marāṭhī, etc.) on paper in all of north India, *śāradā* (which is no longer used) on the bark of birch in Kashmir, bangālī (in use for Bengalī) on paper and palm leaf in Bengal, Oriya (in use for Oriya) on palm leaves in Orissa, Telugu (in use for Telugu) on palm leaves in Andhra and in Tamil Nadu, *grantha* (of which an abridged version serves Tamil) on palm leaves in Tamil Nadu, Kannaḍa (in use for Kannaḍa) on palm leaves in Karnataka, Malayālī (in use for Malayālam) on palm leaves in Kerala, etc. The Arabic script has sometimes been used for Sanskrit during the Mogul period.

All these scripts, being derived from the same prototype, follow the same principle. This principle has been elaborated following the phonetic analysis of Sanskrit made by the ancient grammarians. It provides a sign for each phoneme and each sign has only one pronunciation. The graphic sign is called *akṣara*. There are simple *akṣaras* for writing a vowel when it constitutes a syllable by itself or a consonant pronounced with the sound *a*. The others are compounds of a simple consonantal *akṣara* and a secondary sign to cancel the vowel *a* (case of the consonant standing by itself) or to add a vowel other than *a*, and finally combinations of several consonantal signs reduced in size, at times altered in their form, placed on either side or superimposed and serving to write groups of consonants. This writing then enables one to write all the phonemes of a string accurately, either as separate consonants and vowels or, what is most frequent, syllable by syllable.

CHAPTER II

REPRESENTATIONS OF SANSKRIT AND THE PHILOSOPHY OF SPEECH

Linguistic awareness has from the very beginning been accompanied by reflections and speculations on speech. They were directed first to the Vedic language, then to classical Sanskrit, and incidentally to other languages. The philosophy of speech is thus in India practically a 'philosophy of Sanskrit'. In order to understand the exceptional status given to this language it is necessary first to recall how its relationship with other languages was seen.

I. Sanskrit and other languages

The multiplicity of languages is a problem that the Sanskrit man of letters had necessarily to face, because even from a very early period Sanskrit was always used in the midst of other languages. He has, it seems, never taken this reality as a curse, not even as a misfortune. There is no myth like that of the Tower of Babel in India. The difference in languages is on the contrary well accepted and turned to advantage for the development of culture. We have seen that

Sanskrit was made flexible by its users to help it borrow and assimilate the loanwords. One explanation given for the multiplicity of languages is the diversification of Sanskrit by corruption (*apabhraṃśa*) in the various classes of society and the various other regions of the world. But a more sophisticated view appears also, based on the recognition of the social, literary and religious value of other languages, they having become in their turn the subject matter of reflection by the grammarians. It is the case of the Middle Indian languages. The Sanskrit grammarians did not fail to notice the resemblance of these languages to Sanskrit. They do not generally speak of a derivational relationship, as established by modern historical grammar between Old Indo-Aryan and Middle Indian. Furthermore, they do not dissociate the Vedic language from classical Sanskrit. Hence it is this language alone which is treated as the basis (*prakṛti*) for all others. The notion of *prakṛti* is not here that of a matrix which undergoes a transformation. Rather, it is the notion of a fixed model from which one can understand and describe partial imitations and, incidentally, modifications of any importance. A certain number of Middle Indian languages have been described in this way by Sanskrit grammarians. They call them 'prākrit' *prākṛta*, a word which means literally 'derived from a *prakṛti*', to be understood mainly as 'described according to the Sanskrit model'. The earliest Prākrit grammars come long after that of Pāṇini. They borrow from him all of their terminology and are themselves composed in Sanskrit, in brief formulas of the same style. They are manuals enabling one to shift from Sanskrit to Prākrit, hence highlighting the differences. The Pāli of the Buddhist Scriptures has been described by Kaccāyana still later, in an apparently more independent fashion, because it is presented independently and its grammar is composed in Pāli. However this grammar is also strongly inspired by the Sanskrit grammars and the Pāli language is understood there from the structures designed for Sanskrit.

The Dravidian languages constitute in India a totally different family from the Indo-European. One might expect to find a conception and descriptions of them that are clearly independent of those of Sanskrit. While the oldest Tamil grammar, *Tolkāppiyam*, is in fact very independent, although not completely escaping the influence of Sanskrit, its successors choose to be influenced by the Sanskrit grammarians, borrow their terminology from them, and overlay the Dravidian with purely Indo-Aryan structures like composition, derivation, etc. Kannaḍa and Telugu grammars are composed in Sanskrit. In this case also Sanskrit is regarded rather as a model, and not as an origin. For example, the great Kannaḍa grammarian, Bhaṭṭākalaṅka (late sixteenth century), composed a grammar of his language in Sanskrit, very closely imitating the Paninian model, but he defended a view in which Sanskrit is considered as just a language among others, Kannaḍa being in the same class. He belonged to the Jaina religion, possessed a very high culture in three languages, the Ardhamāgadhī of the Jaina Scriptures, Sanskrit and his mother tongue Kannaḍa. He envisaged the existence of an eternal language which was that of 'the omniscient Lord, from whose lips the Word emanated, in the form of all languages'. He distinguished 18 major languages from 700 minor ones, the former being those in which the sages of his religion spoke. As far as he was concerned Sanskrit was on the same level as Kannaḍa with regard to the one and only speech of the Lord. He admitted that Sanskrit was fit to be taught, because, according to him, correct and incorrect forms are distinguished in that language, that is to say because it had a grammar. But the same quality was shared by other languages, including Kannaḍa. As regards the relation between these various languages, forms of the transcendent word of the Lord, he did not see it from a historical or evolutionary perspective. He described it poetically as the differentiated manifestation of the same matter: 'As the rain fallen from the sky at the time of the monsoon, although one and with one taste, according as it reaches a saline, black or arid field assumes different natures, namely water with saltish, sweet, or astringent taste, ..., likewise the word of the Lord, although a single speech at its birth, undifferentiated like the sound of the waves, is transformed into the different languages when it reaches the region of the ear of the various hearers.'

II. The place given to Sanskrit in the world and in society

The geographical distribution of the languages has also been the subject of reflection by Indian grammarians. The Prākrits are named according to their place of use: Mahārāṣṭrī, Śaurasenī, etc. Perhaps this corresponded to a reality in the beginning. But these languages were soon cultivated for a literary or religious purpose which separated them from living usage and led to their expansion. Their names and their geographical associations are however retained.

There are Indian mythical geographies which distribute the space of the universe into levels inhabited by various species of celestial, terrestrial, and subterranean beings. In this context Sanskrit is given as the language of the gods dwelling in the various heavens. It is often called *amara-*

vāṇī, a compound word with a double meaning 'immortal speech' and 'speech of the immortals'. The correct language is said to be that of the gods. When a grammarian admits to not being able to decide if a contentious form is correct or not, he says that one must appeal to Indra, king of the gods. Now, the brahmin is said to be a 'god on earth'. It follows therefore that Sanskrit is accepted as a language of the terrestrial world too, but only as a language of the brahmins. It is also the language of other categories of beings, such as a demon like Rāvaṇa, and a monkey like Hanumān. But they are heroes. Sanskrit appears thus always in the position of language of the higher species, classes and individuals.

This is a mythological conception of things. It is not reality, not even a legal rule. The *dharma-śāstra* which is the depository discipline of social rules, law, customs, etc. does not reserve Sanskrit for the exclusive use of the brahmin class. It reserves the recitation of the Vedas (*svādhyāya*) to the men of the three higher classes, the 'twice-born', because they receive a form of sacrament (*saṃskāra*) which renders them fit for undertaking this study, seen as a religious rite and duty for which the responsibility lies with professionals. But as regards the general study and use of the Sanskrit language for all other purposes, it does not seem that there was any restriction on any category. Tradition testifies to cases of very advanced knowledge and mastery of the language acquired by non-brahmins or by women. In the Sanskrit grammatical literature there is a considerable portion of works from which the rules specific to the Vedas and useful only to the professional reciters are excluded, because manuals were required in large numbers for the general study of Sanskrit. If in reality it is observed that the majority of the Sanskrit men of letters are brahmins, that is the result of particular circumstances of the history of Indian society, and not because of any rule. The representation of the social status of Sanskrit in the consciousness of the users is that it is the language of the educated people, and nothing more, but not the language of birth into a class.

III. Sanskrit and the transcended speech

The idea of deified or transcended speech appears from the oldest times. Generally speech and Sanskrit are equated. Sanskrit from this point of view is no longer a tongue, but language itself. The name 'Sanskrit' itself is not applied to this concept of transcended speech. But the transcended speech is inferred from the data provided by Sanskrit. It would be correct to describe this process of thought as a philosophy of speech rather than simple religious speculation, because it is a process of reasoning based on the technique of the *vyākaraṇa* that also seeks to account for the psychological and mystical aspirations of the followers of what was first the Vedic, then the Hindu, religion. Furthermore, the *vaiyākaraṇas*, or expert grammarians, of the Paninean school have been recognised in the Indian tradition as having constituted a branch of philosophy, a *darśana*, that is to say a metaphysical system founded on a technique and leading to a doctrine of salvation. Three stages can be identified in their thinking: a scientific analysis consisting in the determination of the expressive element in speech; the elaboration, always by the use of logical reasoning, of a subtle, transcendent form of the gross speech, or a sort of reductionist search for the essence of speech from phenomena; and the framing of a discipline of language, a discipline that purifies the subject in his entire person.

1. Sanskrit, the eternal word

The idea of eternity appears in Kātyāyana and Patañjali through the use of the word *siddha* 'already realised' with which they qualify the language which they describe. This term corresponds to the idea that the language is received as a heritage from elders, in other words parents and teachers who themselves received it from their elders. No inheritor creates. If he innovates, it is a corruption. The correct language is already created, already there, when it is used. As far back as human memory will carry us, it has always had this status. It cannot be imagined as having been created at any initial point in time. The idea of the absence of creation leads directly to the idea of eternity. Thus the correct (*sādhu*) language, that is to say not corrupted by a human innovation, is eternal. And because the grammarian does not create words, but only accounts for the structure of those that already exist by his teaching, that language whose structures he describes is the eternal, correct language. Patañjali illustrates this idea by an example:

> 'How does one know that the word, its meaning, and their relation are already established (that is to say eternal)? By an example from daily life. In daily life we employ the words after having learnt their meaning, we do not try to create them. For example someone has to use a pot. He goes to a potter and says to him: "make me a pot; I have something to have to do with it." But he who wishes to use words does not go to a grammarian to tell him: "make me words; I have to use them." Only after having learnt their meaning does he employ words.'

The same conception is attached to the texts of the Vedas and to other sacred texts. It has been seen that the Vedas were transmitted orally and by memorisation from master to disciple. They are an age-old heritage and are not seen as having been created, since they have always been inherited. They are therefore held to be eternal. They are called *āgama* 'tradition', literally 'that which comes [from a master]' or *śruti* 'hearing' because they are not obtained otherwise than by having been heard from the lips of a master. The fact that the Vedas are seen as eternal implies that their language is itself eternal.

2. The transcended word

The Vedic poets were the first philosophers of speech. They went directly to the conception of a transcendent speech. Speech is the main instrument of the ritual of invocation of the divinities to whom they address their offerings thrown into the sacrificial fire. The ritual formula appeared to them to have a hidden effectiveness that distinguished it from ordinary speech. They were interested in enigmas, and this type of speech with hidden meaning, the subject of verbal tournaments, is one of the first entities to which they applied the word *brahman*. We know the rich connotations that this term acquired in Indian philosophy. It is in the power of the word that Indians have approached the concept of the absolute. Having regard, then, to the admirable power attributed to speech, it was soon presented as being more than an efficient tool, as being an entity external to man which comes to him, a divinity which will endow him with strength (*Ṛgveda* VIII.100.11):

devī́ṃ vā́cam ajanayanta devā́s tā́ṃ viśvárūpāḥ paśávo vadanti |
sā́ no mandréṣam ū́rjaṃ dúhānā dhenúr vā́g asmā́n úpa súṣṭutaítu ||

'The deities generated the Goddess Speech, and beings of every figure speak her.
May She, the Gladdener, yielding food and vigour, the Milch-cow Speech, approach us, meetly lauded.'

Patañjali was first and foremost the commentator of Pāṇini's *sūtras* and an expert in the formation of words. But he had been led on occasions to define more and more inclusive linguistic concepts and had encountered important problems which could not be sidestepped, in particular the problem of the relationship between sound and meaning. What produces the presence of a cognition in the mind, when a sound is heard by the ear? Language shares in two natures, the sound and the mind. Its status is to be defined. Patañjali affirmed clearly the role of the mind. The sounds are produced in succession in the spoken chain. The representation of the succession of sounds is something mental. It does not belong to the sounds themselves, since they are never produced simultaneously. Must one therefore regard speech as a pure representation of the mind? Patañjali did not present such a thesis at all. On the contrary he introduced into Indian thought a concept of an essence of speech which is neither the physical sound, nor the mind, but a third specific entity of speech. He called it by the name *sphoṭa* whose meaning is twofold: 'that which is manifested' and 'that which manifests'. The *sphoṭa* is that which is manifested in the mind by the sound through the agency of hearing, and that which manifests the meaning in the mind. Patañjali spoke only incidentally and very briefly of it while explaining how Pāṇini mentions phonemes. When a phoneme *a* is mentioned in a rule, for example in *ato bhisa ais* 'after *a ais* replaces *bhis*', it is a word whose meaning is its own form. Is this form the sound as it was uttered by the speaker of the formula or also all the other possible realisations of it? To this question Patañjali replied that the phoneme uttered *a* has as its meaning the *sphoṭa* of this word, but not the particular form pronounced in the formula. He did not resort to the idea of a class of *a* defined by a common trait, but to the idea that there was an element common to all the different forms in which this word could be heard so as to procure the comprehension of all the possible *a*. He added that this common element, manifested and manifester (*sphoṭa*), was speech itself, since sound was only a property of speech: *sphoṭaḥ śabdaḥ* | *dhvaniḥ śabdaguṇaḥ*. It amounted to asserting that speech was not in essence sound, and neither was it a psychological phenomenon. Its essence could not be reduced to matter, or mind. Patañjali passes here to the philosophical plane of reflection. He succeeds in considering the essence of speech as being something else than sound, a different specific entity, capable of assuming an auditory manifestation, and comprehended by the mind. He then remembers the Vedic verses such as *Ṛgveda* I.164.45:

> *catvā́ri vā́k párimitā padā́ni tā́ni vidur brāhmaṇā́ yé manīṣíṇaḥ* |
> *gúhā trī́ṇi níhitā néṅgayanti turī́yaṃ vācó manuṣyā̀ vadanti* ||
>
> 'There are four demarcated portions of speech. The brahmins who control their mind know them. Three [quarters], being kept in a hidden place, do not have any movement. Humans speak the fourth [quarter] of speech.'

According to him the first line of this verse refers to the knowledge of grammar. The four portions of speech are the noun, the verb, the verbal prefix and the particle. Educated persons, here called 'brahmins who control their mind', know them, they are the grammarians. The second line of the verse is no longer about these very obvious grammatical categories, but about the four quarters [of speech] of which three are hidden. The idea of hidden and of absence of movement is explained by Patañjali by the metaphor of absence of blinking of eyes. This is a characteristic trait of the gods in Indian mythology. In the context of Indian culture this imagery suggests the divine nature of speech.

Bhartṛhari (5th century AD?) received Patañjali's heritage. We are indebted to him for a commentary on the *Mahābhāṣya*, partly lost, and an original work on the philosophy of language entitled *Vākyapadīya*. The first part of the *Vākyapadīya* is a metaphysics of correct speech, that is to say Sanskrit such as the *vyākaraṇa* constructs it. He employs especially the term *śabda* for the essence of speech. His *śabda* does not differ in the main from the *sphoṭa* of Pāṇini. It is indeed an essence which is neither matter nor mind. From the beginning of his work he gives it the most exalted status, that of the absolute principle (*brahman*):

anādinidhanaṃ brahma śabdatattvaṃ yad akṣaram |
vivartate 'rthabhāvena prakriyā jagato yataḥ ||

'The reality of speech is the eternal *brahman*, without beginning or end; out of it emanates the creation of the universe in the form of meaning.'

This text asserts on the one hand that speech is a reality in its essence and on the other hand that this reality is the absolute principle, referred to by the word *brahman*. This word is the principal designation of the abstract principle of all things, of the absolute, of reality at its ultimate level, of pure consciousness envisaged as subject isolated from all objects, of God in His most abstract form. It is here applied to speech which thus receives the highest metaphysical status. We note finally in Bhartṛhari's formula the affirmation of the primacy of speech in relation to meaning. Speech is the first reality, without beginning, or end; meaning, that is to say knowledge, emanates from it and has an origin in it; the visible universe emanates from knowledge. We know of other doctrines in India such as *advaita-vedānta*, and tantric schools for example, where speech is a second reality in relation to consciousness, where it is named *śabda-brahman* '*speech*-brahman', second in relation to *brahman* as such, which is the first and defined as consciousness. For the philosopher-linguist speech has the highest status of absolute *brahman* and consciousness is but its manifestation.

3. Sanskrit as a way to religious salvation

It is as grammarians that the philosophers of speech conceived of a path of salvation. Their goal is the awareness of the undifferentiated principle that speech or *brahman* is. It is in the language which he possesses in himself that the subject will have to seek this awareness. The study of the language is itself the means of approach to the *sphoṭa-brahman*. The awareness of the structures taught in grammar is the starting point of this quest. It is necessary to first discern that which is corruption brought by man to the given eternal language. Grammar is the instrument of this discrimination and hence a factor in the purification of the knowledge of speech. Once the knowledge is purified of all corruptions, the subject can comprehend speech in its eternal essence, understand its undifferentiated nature by a process of reducing the differences, and arrive at an awareness of speech as the principle, namely the absolute *brahman*. This process of awareness of the non-difference by reducing the differences is a psychological operation which came under Yoga. And in this fashion the *vaiyākaraṇas* are much like the Yogins in the matter of discipline. This likeness is, no doubt, at the origin of the tradition which considers the commentator of Pāṇini and the author of *Yogasūtra*, both bearing the name of

Patañjali, as incarnations of the eternal mythical serpent called Śeṣa. The way of *vyākaraṇa* is a way of Yoga. And when a philosopher like Bhartṛhari speaks of the ideal of liberation he does not hesitate to assert:

> '[Grammar is] ... the door of freedom, the medicine for the diseases of language, the purifier of all sciences; it sheds its light on them; ... it is the first rung on the ladder that leads up to realisation of supernatural powers, and the straight royal road for those who seek freedom.'

Recall that for philosophers like Bhartṛhari and most of his successors, the grammar envisaged is that of the trinity Pāṇini, Kātyāyana and Patañjali, and the purifying and redeeming language is the Sanskrit produced (*saṃskṛta*) by this grammar.

CHAPTER III

THE USERS OF SANSKRIT

I. Sanskrit as everyday language

One often distinguishes between popular language and scholarly language. Sanskrit is known to us as a scholarly language by through abundant documentation. But a fully popular language which would not be dependent on the authority of grammarians and men of letters eludes us, for want of evidence. It may be freely supposed that Old Indo-Aryan was used for the purposes of ordinary communication in life, before evolving into Middle Indian or into the Sanskrit of the grammarians. But such a state of the language is barely documented for the historian. One has to search for it in the Vedic texts. These are poems of essentially religious inspiration and texts of ritual techniques. They are a document on the language used by the specialists of ceremonial. To what extent this language differed from the popular language can in no way be determined, because no comparison is possible. We have seen the evolution of Vedic, entrusted to the care of the learned and the grammarians, and that of the Old Indo-Aryan fostered by people of the various different provinces and social levels, leading to the big difference between the types of Middle Indian that have been attested and Sanskrit. Must one then speak of a divorce between the language of an intellectual class and that of the people? That would be putting it too simply. For the two types of language always continue to coexist and are always in a position to influence each other. They must often have coexisted in the same individual, in the man of letters who has as his mother tongue an Indo-Aryan or Dravidian language and masters Sanskrit, and in him who is not a professional but has some knowledge of Sanskrit in addition to his mother tongue. The professional man of letters could be using his language at two levels, a technical level and a more natural level.

Who were the non-professionals using Sanskrit, and at what level did they use it? On this point there is evidence, namely the multilingual Indian theatre. There are dramatic works in which the characters speak different languages according to their social class. In these plays we see brahmins, kings and nobles speak Sanskrit and converse with representatives of other classes speaking various Prakrits. Theatre has a major element of convention, and convention does not necessarily reflect reality. What is to be remembered is the status of Sanskrit not so much as the language of high society, but rather as the language of those who have access to higher education. Even in the nobility, women speak Prakrit. The jester, confidant of the king, is a brahmin who does not speak Sanskrit and who makes himself an object of ridicule among other things by his lack of learning in the Vedas. We must not however carry this portrayal of the unlearned too far. The characters who do not speak Sanskrit do still understand it, and therefore have a minimum of learning. And there is communication between different languages. This is not a totally improbable or unreal situation. Multilingualism is a remarkable feature of Indian society, much more widespread in India than in Europe. Theatrical convention merely highlights it.

Another noteworthy example is the Sanskrit literature of religious instruction, e.g. hagiographies, legends of sacred places, mythological accounts, etc. Their authors are learned, as testified by the refined language of the texts. This literature is very abundant and is addressed to a vast public of the Faithful. Must one conclude from this that there is among all the Faithful a knowledge and capacity to understand Sanskrit, and see users of Sanskrit in the people as a whole who practise Hinduism? It is certain that this literature truly addressed to the people implies that they are to some extent familiar with Sanskrit. One cannot however exaggerate this. The level of knowledge can vary from one individual to another, from one group to another, from one region to another. We note a desire for simplifying the style. We must also consider the means used for disseminating these texts. The principal means is not the document, printed or handwritten. There have always been in all regions of India professional reciters of mythological texts. Their function is to recite and comment, the commentary being made in the most widely understood local language. The Sanskrit text is not neglected. Each verse is chanted or sung. The narrator often has an acolyte who asks previously planned questions which serve as an introduction to the commentaries in the local language. The narrator resorts to song, and even dance, to enliven his descriptions. We have here an art whose function is to disseminate the Sanskrit text. We also see by this example that while there are texts that vouch for the existence of an audience, we cannot conclude directly from this that this audience had an advanced knowledge of or a familiarity with Sanskrit.

II. The Sanskrit man of letters, or pandit

We cannot imagine Sanskrit without the professional men of letters who cultivated it. It is they who are its major users. We must define their profession and determine the place that the language occupied within it.

Throughout its history India has been able to ensure for its intellectual professionals conditions of living that enabled them to devote themselves fully to their vocation. The continuity of intellectual activity has thus been maintained without interruption, with examples of transmission of knowledge across many millennia. The most constant feature in this is the use of Sanskrit. It would not be wrong to define this language by its close relationship with intellectual activity in all its forms in India and, as we shall see, in a major part of Asia. The generic name of 'pandit' (*paṇḍita*) is given to a person who exercises his profession, or has acquired great mastery of some intellectual activity, by using Sanskrit. In the second place the use of this term is extended to the scholar who masters a provincial language of India, such as Tamil, etc., and uses it as the Sanskrit pandit uses his language. Nevertheless, it is a fact that the pandit is characterised by an intellectual training in which Sanskrit plays the primary role, even if he cultivates another language.

We must not equate the pandit with the brahmin. The brahmin is defined by his birth and by his religious obligations, while the pandit is defined by his intellectual training alone. Most brahmins are not pandits and there are pandits who are not brahmins. The earliest Indian intellectuals whose memories and works have come down to us are the Vedic poets. Patañjali is the model of the classical pandit and he has himself taken care to describe his ideal. The study of

Sanskrit is still alive today. And one can meet Sanskrit pandits who have the will to preserve their cultural heritage, not only by distant observation from without, as one studies an extinct civilisation, but by living this culture, by engaging their whole being within this framework.

1. The Vedic poet

The oldest literary monuments of India, the hymns of the *Ṛgveda*, testify by their volume and their quality to the existence of masters of the word. We know practically nothing about them, not even their names. The names of sages to whom tradition attributes the authorship of these hymns are rather the names of the families that had preserved them from generation to generation. But the authors of these hymns sometimes describe their condition and their activities. What they say is enough to give us a glimpse of poets who live by the power of their speech. Their works are prayers addressed to the divinities of the Vedic pantheon and used in liturgy. The solemn rites of the oldest form of religion are based on offerings of milk and butter made into the fire and addressed to the deities, invoked by the poems and informed through prayers of the human desires to be fulfilled in return. Speech is thus the major tool in the success of the sacrifice. It has an effectual power which does not appear in everyday use, but which is known to the most skilful, the most inspired, and which is the object of the search and the discovery of the poet. The poet is, then, a practitioner of the sacrifice. Since the great Vedic sacrifices required considerable human and material resources to carry them out, they were financed by persons having the necessary resources and executed by the professionals. The poets were among the latter. They formed some kind of select circles, helping mutually or competing with each other, expecting from an initial success fresh commissions and glorifying their group by their success. Their efforts were sometimes directed to speech itself, to the pursuit of the mysterious power that it contained. The *bráhman*, as we saw, refers to this power of the speech and they organised some kind of verbal tournaments (*brahmodya*) in which the participants posed riddles to each other, competing with each other in the act of expressing *bráhman*. The qualities sought after were inspiration, thoughts couched in refined language (*dhi*), quickness of wit and ability to improvise. He who succeeds is said to possess the *bráhman*. He becomes a model for others and his influence on the language is recognised. 'As much extensive as *bráhman* is, so much great is speech'. We see that right from the beginning of the Indian tradition the collegiality of a profession of speech is recognised with the idea of a responsibility in its constitution. The Vedic poet is the prototype of the grammarian man of letters of the classical period.

2. The traditional pandit

We have described above the role of Patañjali whose language, methods of intellectual work and exposition became a model for future generations of pandits. The qualification of 'traditional' is often attached to the pandit who follows this model, in the sense that his learning is not the result of an artificial and bookish reconstitution of an antiquated knowledge, but that there is reason to think that this knowledge and especially this style and intellectual way of life, have been transmitted from master to disciple, through example, across the ages, with almost unbroken continuity. We have seen (p. 34) the description that Patañjali gives of the Sanskrit man of letters whom he calls *śiṣṭa* 'educated'. The geographical and social situation that he gives them are those of his period. That will change subsequently, as Sanskrit spread in all of South India and far outside its borders. And Patañjali himself recognises the excellence of the Sanskrit of some non-brahmins, when he tells us of the defeat of a grammarian by his coachman who corrected him. The other traits survive across the ages. The cachet 'who has a good stock of grains' indicates the most frequent condition enabling a man of letters to be free from material concerns, in other words that of a landed proprietor living off the income from a farm. The other epithets describe the qualities of intelligence and psychological discipline which will always be extolled and cultivated.

A) The training of the pandit

While a near spontaneous 'effortless' learning is seen as being achievable by birth into one of the good *śiṣṭa* families described by Patañjali, it has also been the subject of considerable efforts which have led to the dissemination of Sanskrit over a vast territory and with two thousand years of success. From a very early date these efforts were accompanied by a profound reflection and by a remarkable awareness of the possibilities of psychological formation. For the Indian philosophers understood very early the role of the unconscious in psychic activity and have knowingly worked to shape the personality by influencing the unconscious. This is apparent in the notions of *vāsanā* and *saṃskāra* which in their psychological aspect are already attested in the period of the *Upaniṣads*. The starting idea is that no experience

—deed and related cognition, influence on the awareness, sentiment, concept, etc.— once lived, is ever irretrievably lost. It leaves a trace in the psyche. No experience is innocent. And the psyche is compared to a box in which a sweet-smelling substance had been placed and then removed. The fragrance remains. Similarly, the lived experience leaves an invisible, but real, trace called *vāsanā*. These traces do not remain in a chaotic state within the psyche. They organise themselves and so construct a personality, prepare the individual for new experiences, enable him, for example, to remember and make him capable of new psychological activities. This psychological preparation by the traces of the earlier experiences is called *saṃskāra*. This is the term which is at the origin of the name of Sanskrit, the language which has received the *saṃskāra*, in other words the preparation by grammar with a view to a more skilful use. *Saṃskāra* is any preparation of something with a view to an activity, all that must be done to endow a thing with the ability to function. What has been thought of for the language has also been thought of for the human psyche. We see the importance of the application of such a notion to education. For if one knows that the traces of experience organise themselves, one can then think of prescribing experiences with a view to constituting a stock of traces which will be the material for the organisation of the psyche of an individual. One can first constitute the matter that will go into the personality. One can go further by directing the organisation of this matter towards definite activities by creating a *saṃskāra*, a 'preparation' for these activities. The two methods favoured by the education designed in this psychological context are the memorisation of texts, in other words the constitution of a material of traces or *vāsanā*, and the training in the typical intellectual operations of the grammarians, exegetes and logicians, which is the formation of the *saṃskāra*. With this training the pandit will be capable of creation in literary, philosophical, etc. matters. The pandit will be formed psychologically when he has in his learning a data base and the rules of organisation, which will have conferred on him creativity.

The constituents of the knowledge that must be placed in the mind of the future pandit are first the language, next entire texts, and lastly the techniques of grammar (*vyākaraṇa*), exegesis (*mīmāṃsā*) and logic (*nyāya*). These techniques are often grouped together under the name *śāstra* 'teaching', of the word (*pada*), of the sentence (*vākya*) and of the means of correct knowledge (*pramāṇa*). A common course comprises the memorisation of the *Amarakośa*, a versified lexicon of words categorised by synonyms, the *sūtras* of Pāṇini and Kātyāyana with their appendices, lists of roots, etc., *sūtras* or manuals of *mīmāṃsā* and *nyāya*, a manual of poetics, a certain number of literary masterpieces and a great mass of sayings, formulas, verses, moral and dialectical expedients, whose authors are unknown, and which are the oral tradition of the Sanskrit schools. This is a base which is designed to be complemented by the memorisation of a branch of the Veda, the study in depth of one or several *śāstras* or of some other discipline, such as *dharma-śāstra* or teaching of the Law and of the customs, mythology (*Mahābhārata*, *Rāmāyaṇa*, *Purāṇas*), *Tantra* or techniques of the religious rituals, medicine, etc. to cite only the most common ones.

The Sanskrit pandits favour oral teaching. One reason for this is the psychological objective. The direct contact with the master as opposed to the isolation of reading, the greater difficulty of memorising by hearing alone, which requires the unflagging attention to the word of the master, whereas the eyes can be more easily taken off the written matter, then returned to it, and several features of this kind show that oral teaching carried out without the aid of writing achieves a stronger psychological impression. There are teachers who as a matter of honour do not use books. Writing is excluded as a rule, at least for the transmission of the Veda. A saying makes fun of the science which is in the books: it is like the money in another's pocket; one does not have it in hand in case of need.

That does not mean that writing was not used. While the pandits accomplish feats of memory, they are not averse to the use of books that can usefully supplement human memory. The teaching of scripts is a part of primary education. Among the pandits there is a category specialised in this art. Before the very slow introduction of printing from Europe in the sixteenth century, publication was effected only through manuscripts, which rendered necessary the profession of scribe (*kāyastha, lekhaka*). And from the period when the use of writing spread for writing down Sanskrit, in other words after the Christian era, there was a category of pandits whose usual occupation was copying manuscripts. The engraving of inscriptions on stone and copperplate was another activity, entrusted to artisan-sculptors (*śilpin*); a number of medieval inscriptions bear two signatures, that of the author of the text and that of the engraver.

In the ideal model, often described in literature, teaching is done generally in the family setting whether it be the disciple's own family or that of the master (*guru-kula*). There is a distinction between the master who gives the sacraments of Hinduism and the masters who are entrusted with intellectual training. In some cases they can be one and the same person, in others they are separate. The name of *guru* is preferred for the former, that of *upādhyāya* for the latter; and *ācārya* is used for both at a more advanced level. The disciple is as a rule taken care of by the master. A religious ceremony (*upanayana*) solemnises the beginning of the studies and the stay with the master. This ceremony is said to be a second birth, called *brahma-janman* 'birth into the *brahman*', the term *brahman* connoting here the essence of speech, the Vedic texts and pure knowledge, a birth in which the mother is Sāvitrī, the deified Vedic speech, and the father the *ācārya*... As a rule the three classes of brahmins, kṣatriyas and vaiśyas are eligible to receive the sacrament. That is why they are called generically *dvi-ja* 'the twice-born'. Furthermore, this ceremony is said to be a *saṃskāra*; for it is a ritual which 'prepares' the disciple for entering the active life whose first stage is education. The disciple is called *brahma-cārin* 'one who practises the *brahman*', where the word *brahman* has the same connotations, with in addition that of corporal, psychological and moral discipline of *tapas* 'asceticism'. Among the virtues required of the disciple figures chastity, connoted by the word *brahma-carya* which by extension refers to this condition of the student. The life of the disciple in the 'family of the master' (*guru-kula*) includes material service to the master in addition to the hearing of his teaching, and studying on one's own (*svādhyāya*). We see here the total character of the education, material, affective, social, intellectual, moral and spiritual. The profound nature of the intellectual training and the concern for treating it not as a superficial acquisition of knowledge, but as a profound transformation of the psyche, a psychological *saṃskāra*, is revealed by a definition given by Kauṭilya of the method of acquisition of knowledge in eight psychological states of the disciple: desire to listen to the word of the master (*śuśrūṣā*) which implies the attention focussed on everything that emerges from his lips; the hearing of this word (*śravaṇa*) with the same implication of attention, the apprehending by the mind (*grahaṇa*); the memorisation (*dhāraṇa*); the reflection, consisting in seeking the applications and the non-applications of the teaching (*ūha-apoha*); the refined comprehension of the contents of the teaching with conceptualisation and discrimination of the nuances (*artha-vijñāna*); the complete entry into the reality of the meaning (*tattva-abhiniveśa*). The differentiation made between the last mentioned states brings out the aspect of psychological permeation aimed at for the acquisition of knowledge.

In actual practice the *guru-kula* can be the real family of a master, or in a wider sense a centre of teaching. Sanskrit literature contains a number of descriptions of residences (*āśramas*) of great masters, forest hermitages where the disciples crowd round a venerated master surrounded by a number of tutors. The remote location outside towns and built up areas, the wild, natural setting of the education centres, is a constant ideal in the Indian tradition. One can still find it being pursued in the modern establishments such as the Santiniketan university in Bengal founded by the poet Tagore, and even some state universities established recently. Historical documents bear evidence to the existence of centres of very great importance down to the early Middle Ages. We shall cite by way of example that of Nālandā, a Buddhist centre from very old times, which acquired a great influence towards the 3rd and 4th centuries AD with the presence of the *ācāryas* Nāgārjuna and his disciple Asaṅga and which would from then on be the major centre of the Mahāyāna school until the disappearance of Buddhism from India. We know of this centre, and can appreciate its importance, on the one hand by its description given by the Chinese pilgrim Hiuan-tsang (602-664) after having visited it, on the other by recent archaeological research which has excavated the site and has uncovered imposing ruins. The centre could accommodate more than 10,000 permanent residents. There were 1,500 teachers for 8,500 students. The course of study included the Sanskrit *śāstras*, grammar, etc. and the Buddhist Scriptures and philosophy. The student aspiring for the highest level had to take a tough entrance examination and follow a course of study lasting some fifteen years between the ages of 15 and 30. The centre used to be visited by a large number of masters and scholarly debates took place regularly in which philosophical and religious doctrines, heretical or orthodox, confronted each other.

The teaching was as a rule free. The master who demanded a regular salary was despised and the prohibition on selling knowledge was often pronounced. The disciple in fact put himself at the material service of his master during his stay under his roof and could then engage himself into some activities that helped the community to subsist. He is described in the literature as at times going to beg for food, according to the Buddhist ideal for example, or going into the forest to gather fruits and roots, firewood, etc. Lastly tradition required the disciple to make a ritual gift (*dakṣiṇā*) to the master at the end of his studies. The great centres obviously depended on charitable endowments, royal or other.

B) The living conditions and functions of the pandit

At the end of his studies the new pandit could take a vow of celibacy and pursue his ascetic discipline of study by remaining in the same hermitage or institution in which he was educated. He was then called *naiṣṭhika*. This was generally the mode of recruitment of the pontiffs and administrators of religious institutions. Hinduism is essentially a religion of lay people, but it does not ignore institutions of a monastic nature, which are called *āśramas* or *maṭhas*. Even though their forms differ in the extreme, the major and most traditional ones are composed of monks who have taken the vows of *saṃnyāsa* 'total renunciation' and whose vocation is teaching, the propagation of religion, the management of the church by giving directives to the temples for example, the spiritual guidance of the Faithful, the personal study of the *śāstras* and religious texts, the spiritual discipline of the yoga, etc. Sanskrit owes much to these institutions, because historically they were the most stable and it is they who were best able to ensure the continuity of the transmission of knowledge and the quality of formation of the personalities of the pandits. We shall cite just one example among many others, the *maṭha* of Śṛṅgeri in Karnāṭaka. It is believed to be founded by the great non-dualist philosopher, Śaṃkara, in the 8th century AD. It was endowed by the Emperor of Vijayanagar, Harihara II (1377-1404), with lands whose revenues were meant to provide for the subsistence of three pandits, Nārāyaṇa Vājapeyin, Pāṇḍuraṅga Dīkṣita and Narahari Somayājin who were entrusted with the responsibility of commenting the four Vedas. This task has been accomplished without interruption since the 15th century in the Vedic and Sanskrit school of this *maṭha*. The present head of this school is Śrī Mūranemane Rāma Bhaṭṭa who is a descendant of Narahari Somayājin. In addition to its traditional school the *maṭha* has a number of social, ritual and other activities and has a great influence on the religious life of all of south India.

On completion of his studies, the pandit could enter the life of householder, establish a family and exercise an intellectual profession. His livelihood would then depend mainly on royal or other form of patronage. He would then stay in a town and could be closely associated with a royal court. He was often endowed with a piece of land whose income would be at his disposal and exempt from all tax. The gifts of lands to brahmins are frequently mentioned in inscriptions on stone or on copperplates, composed in Sanskrit and containing a panegyric of the king or the donor. These gifts are very numerous, made to brahmins as a general rule. Inasmuch as the brahmins were learned and cultivated, they are deeds of patronage. It has frequently been so. Generally the inscription specifies the branch of the Veda to which the brahmin recipient of the endowment belonged. This shows that the intention of the donation was the protection of Vedic culture. Although the three higher classes are entitled to study the Veda and to recite it daily, only the brahmin class was entitled to teach it. This is the reason for the near-monopoly of the brahmins as beneficiaries of these endowments. The donation was hereditary, the brahmins had to keep up the recitation, the practice and the teaching of the Veda from generation to generation. An endowment often brought together brahmins of various Vedic schools. They lived from then on near the lands which brought them income, in the same village or part of town called *agrāhāra*, literally 'food of the best' (frequently spelt *agrahāra*). The establishment of *agrāhāras* has been the most effective means of the expansion of Vedic and Sanskritic culture in the early Middle Ages and of its maintenance in every age. As the *agrāhāras* were located in the cultivated countryside, which in India means a plain irrigated by a river, canals or reservoirs, and as the *maṭhas* were similarly secluded and away from the towns, we can say that the best part of the intellectual activity in India took place in a wild or rural setting.

The first function of the pandit is the daily recitation of the Veda (*svādhyāya*) considered to be a religious rite. It is also the personal study and maintenance of knowledge. The concern for retaining it in memory is ever present. His profession is to place this knowledge at the service of others. Teaching is considered to be a duty. It is said for example that a pandit who has neglected to transmit his learning is reborn after his death into a category of demons called *brahma-rākṣasas* 'demons of learning'. The *rākṣasa* is a demon who watches out for the faults of execution in the rituals conducted by mortals, and, since any mistake is a breach that enables him to enter the sacred enclosure of the ritual, infiltrates the ritual and ruins it. Among these demons the *brahma-rākṣasa* is the most dangerous because he possesses learning, and thus has more ability to find faults.

The pandit is not employed as a temple priest. The priests belong to social groups who have the monopoly of this office. They receive their training as priests in their own circles and some, coming from this background, can pursue studies and be pandits. It is nevertheless true that every pandit by his knowledge of the texts is capable of giving advice, of explaining various matters to priests, and there can be close contact between them. On the other hand a pandit, if he is brahmin, can very often play the role of *purohita*, a common designation of the performer of the sacraments or *saṃskāra*s celebrated in the home of the recipient, such as birth rites, naming ceremonies, initiation (*upanayana*), marriage, funeral rites, etc. The pandits who have memorised a Veda can follow the profession of reciters. The Vedic recitation is supposed to have a purificatory and sanctifying power and is often a supplement to the celebration of a *saṃskāra* or a festival, even though it is not directly a part of the liturgy, simply to bring in auspiciousness. The tantric rite of worship (*pūjā*) of a deity can be celebrated with its own specific formulas not extracted from the Veda and be followed by recitation that is properly Vedic. The reciter is called *pāṭhaka* 'reciter' or *ghana-pāṭhin* 'reciter of the *ghana*' referring to the most complex mode of the art described above (p.21 ff.).

The non-religious functions of a pandit are very diverse. Attached to a royal court he could be court poet entrusted with celebrating the deeds of his employer. The royal panegyric is a genre called *praśasti* in Sanskrit literature. It may be a short work or a long one in high-flown style, either an introduction to a royal charter meant for an inscription, or a long heroic poem. The office of panegyrist could be hereditary. We know of a family at the Vijayanagar court which produced poets who were authors of inscriptions for three generations: Sabhāpati was active between 1514 and 1543, his son Svayaṃbhū was active between 1543 and 1585, his son Rājanātha (attached to a vassal of Madurai, Ativīrarāma Pāṇḍya), and his nephews Kṛṣṇakavi-Kāmakoṭi and Rāma composed inscriptions after 1585. Pandits could be attached to princes or nobles, not always by holding office under them, but by a bond of admiration, not to say friendship, and glorify them in their works. It is for example the case with Bāṇa Bhaṭṭa, one of the most powerful geniuses of Sanskrit literature, who in complete independence sang the exploits of king Harṣa (605-647 AD) of Kanyākubja in a poetic novel 'The epic of Harsa' (*Harṣa-Carita*).

Pandits could enter the state service. Ministers are often brahmin pandits whose orthodoxy as well as learning are equally valued. There is a separate discipline in Sanskrit called *nīti* 'the art of royal behaviour' or *arthaśāstra* 'the science of material achievement' which is the political art and the art of administering a kingdom, as well as ethics. The masterpiece in this genre is the *Arthaśāstra* attributed to Kauṭilya, minister of Candragupta Maurya (?313-289 BC), but possibly compiled later. The administration of justice also had need of pandits learned in the *dharma-śāstra*, a very highly developed branch of Sanskrit literature containing teachings on the Law and on the customs. In this case also pandits can be true officers of the king. We shall cite just one example, of Laṅkaka, brother of the great poet Maṅkhaka, and minister of peace and war of the king of Kashmir, Jayasiṃha (1128-1154 AD), whose talents as a grammarian skilled in the art of commenting on the *Mahābhāṣya* of Patañjali are extolled. That a minister of war should distinguish himself in grammar is unique in the history of the world and could probably happen only in India where this discipline has enjoyed the highest status. There were other pandits who had a more or less distant relationship with the ruling establishment and were consulted on occasions. It is often said that in a contentious matter three pandits were called upon to consider several opposing viewpoints and arrive at the most balanced judgement. And one cannot overemphasise the distant, discreet but effective role which some personalities among the pandits have been able to play. Conversely, royal personages have been able to influence the development of the activities of pandits, not only by protecting them, but also by collaborating in their activities. The history of India has many names of sovereigns who were cultivated and well read, poets and artists, to whom Sanskrit owes also a debt. We may cite the names of King Harṣa (605-647), renowned for three court comedies, the most refined and elegant in Sanskrit drama, of King Bhoja (c.1018-1060) of Central India, to whom is ascribed a very great production of Sanskrit works of the highest level, in various genres, belles-lettres, philosophy and techniques, and always of a powerful originality.

C) Characterisation of the Sanskrit pandit

We have already underscored the major trait of the Sanskrit pandit while talking of his training in the form of building a personality devoted to the use of pure intellect, the psychological constitution being seen as a foundation. The pandit is not a modern researcher who equips himself with materials and outside help for his intellectual tasks. He equips first his mind and his innermost being. External auxiliaries are only his secondary concern.

a) *The oral tradition.* The most characteristic trait of the pandit is his liking for oral communication. We noted this already in respect of the method of teaching. We also noted it by his lack of interest in respect to writing. A very great talent for speech is commonly seen. It is the speech, the quality of orator, which makes the renown of the pandit, more than the distributed book. The great author is traditionally represented as a master who speaks. The ideal model of the creative genius is the mythical figure of the sage Vyāsa to whom is attributed the authorship of the *Mahābhārata*, an epic of some one hundred thousand Sanskrit *ślokas* which are stanzas of 32 syllables, and many other works. He uttered them all from his lips. The task of writing down this immense mass of words was entrusted to Gaṇeśa, a god with the body of a child and with the head of an elephant, son of the divine couple Śiva and Pārvatī. Another mythical figure of poetry is that of Vālmīki, author of the *Rāmāyaṇa*, an epic of 25,000 *ślokas*, which inaugurates the style of great classical Sanskrit poetry and is the foundation of one of the greatest Hindu devotional movements. Vālmīki is presented as the inventor of the epic Sanskrit stanza, called *śloka*. The story goes that he saw a beautiful saras crane pierced by the arrow of a hunter at the moment of its lovemaking. This spectacle moved him to pity. His feelings were expressed spontaneously in a phrase of malediction addressed to the hunter and in a definite rhythm: four times eight syllables with a short vowel not followed by a consonant group in the fifth syllable in the odd lines, in the fifth and the seventh in the even lines. It is the schema of the simplest Sanskrit stanza and was to be universally used in this language. This stanza is a spontaneous speech, a cry from the heart. Literary creation is seen in all of tradition as the direct passage from the thought to the loudly uttered speech. The myth of Vālmīki then goes on to make him pronounce his epic before two young princes, Kuśa and Lava, who are none other than the sons of the hero Rāma of the epic. They become the first bards to go singing from royal court to royal court the heroic deeds of their father. The word *kuśilava* is a common designation for a bard. The tradition of the pandits gives it as the combination of the names of the two princes who initiated the art of epic recitation. We learn from this myth that both the creation and the communication of literature are represented as oral. In this case the myth does not even mention writing.

This characteristic feature of all epic literature has been extended to all other areas in India. In ancient times only the oral and auditory means seem to have been used. It is the case with Pāṇini's *sūtras*. That is apparent in his formalisation. In the modern West the formalisation of a technical language is made mainly with the aid of visual signs, i.e. through writing and graphics, as one can judge by the established model in mathematics. Pāṇini has imagined an ingenious system of markers of the grammatical elements, to indicate the properties and operations which are associated with them. All these markers are auditory and belong to the material of the spoken word. It is for example a phoneme attached to a suffix and indicating that this suffix determines by its presence such and such operation relating to the root: the marker *ñ* of *ya*$^{\tilde{n}}$ indicates that in the root followed by the secondary suffix of family descent there is a *vṛddhi* (*ā*, *ai*, *au*) substitute of the first vowel (*garga* + *ya* > *gārg-ya*). It can be an accent of a vowel: the low tone (*anudātta*) indicates the use of the *ātmanepada* (middle) terminations for a root, the modulated tone (*svarita*) indicates the use of the *parasmaipada* terminations for a verbal root when the fruit of the action goes to a person other than the agent, the use of the *ātmanepada* terminations when it goes to the agent. And furthermore, the marker is identified as such by an auditory sign. In modern transliterations of Pāṇini's text a typographical artifice is employed for recognising a marker which is not an integral part of the morpheme, for example by writing it as a raised letter: *ya*$^{\tilde{n}}$, ^{ṭ}*a*^{c}, ^{ḍu}*pac*^{àṣ}, etc. Pāṇini has no visual symbol. He indicates the vowel used as a marker by a nasalisation: *edh ã*, etc. Both the tone and the adventitious nasalisation have disappeared from use in the post-Patañjalian period. These markers have not been replaced by others but, not being pronounced, their existence had to be indicated. It is not writing that was used for that. To our knowledge the symbols for accent and nasalisation have never been used in manuscripts of grammar. The pandits have on the contrary adopted the habit of mentioning the existence of these properties, after enunciating the element that carries them, in a distinct proposition: *edha spardha... edhādaya udāttā anudāttetaḥ* '*edha, spardha, ...; edha*, etc. have a raised tone and a low tone marker'. In this manner, the Paninean formulas function while being exclusively pronounced and memorised, without being written.

From this point of view, the pandit can be compared to the musician. India possesses a classical music, very scholarly, not simplifiable to a folklore, which requires a great intellectual mastery. The Indian musician is even more exclusive than the pandit vis-à-vis writing. Never has Indian music been written down graphically. The modern musician is averse to making use of the western notation and, while trials for devising a notation have been made, they have scarcely been successful and have never been recognised as an adequate representation of all the tonal features to which the musician attaches importance. On the other hand there exists a tonal and auditory notation for the rhythm of the percussions and the dance. The artists have created for themselves a true language in which each phoneme represents a position of such and such finger on the skin of the drum, with such and such manner of striking, in which the sequence of phonemes gives information on the play of the fingers and, recited, reproduces the rhythm: *dhā dhin dhin dhā / dhā tira kiṭa ṭak'/* ... Dance has a similar language in which each syllable signifies a position of the foot, a flexion of the body, a gesture of the hands and a movement of the eyes, the recited sequence giving the rhythm: *ta ki ta ta ka di mi...* This language of percussions and dance is attested only later. It cannot be very old. The metalanguage of Pāṇini is perhaps its distant ancestor. His principle could naturally have provided the idea for it.

In a general manner the predilection of pandits for oral transmission, and their training in the quality of speech, could only bring them closer to musicians. There are among the pandits singers of the *Sāmaveda*, who have been able to transmit down to the present day the most ancient music known to humanity. And their art of declamation, whether ritual or poetic, is often close to a song. The Sanskrit pandit is close to a musician, contrasting with the Chinese man of letters who by his art of calligraphy is close to the painter.

b) *Memorisation and concentration.* The Sanskrit pandit has often won renown by feats of memorisation. We have spoken of the memorisation of the Vedas, and of the basic manuals of instruction, which aims at the retention in memory of the text in its exact form. There is also another kind of memorisation which is the memorisation of the contents of the texts. This is also an important feature. The pandit, if he does not keep in memory the exact words of an entire text, at least remembers its contents, the order of the exposition, and the place of the ideas and of the various pieces of information in the text. He frequently holds the significant sentences in memory. Lastly, and this is perhaps his most precious treasure, he has in the course of his training stored in his memory a great number of verses, formulas, proverbs, moral aphorisms, witticisms, rules of thought, interpretation procedures, and information of all kinds. And on any occasion he is able to come up with an appropriate quotation. This treasure remains largely oral. One cannot determine how old it is, or from where it came originally. Some elements appear as quotations in texts, but that does not indicate their original source, just their existence in the age-old knowledge of the traditional schools.

Memorisation has the invaluable advantage of making the pandit independent of the external help of books. He is sometimes called a 'living library'. A grammarian, greatly learned in the *Mahābhāṣya* of Patañjali, a very difficult work to assimilate because of its length and its depth of thought, was nicknamed 'walking Mahābhāṣya'. This illustrates best both the pandit's desire and his constant endeavour to be independent of external means. Memorisation is also useful for a simple understanding of complex works. The *Mahābhārata* is probably the longest epic of humanity. Its intrigue is made up of a very complex and long succession of episodes, with a host of protagonists and people, often extraordinary family relationships and ambiguous political relationships, with a lot of unrelated narratives introduced under various pretexts, with lastly the doubling of characters, first celestial then incarnated on earth, and networks of symbols that are to be understood at several levels. The deeper significance of this huge work cannot be understood unless the mind can consider it as a whole as one reads it at its different levels of meaning, that of political intrigue, of war, of the fight between the clans of the Pāṇḍavas and Kauravas which is also that of the gods and the demons, that of the good and the evil, etc. It requires considerable effort to memorise the stories, and the characters who have at times ten different names, for being able to recognise the interesting correlations which make up the value of this masterpiece.

Another example of a text composed for memorisation and which functions well only by this method is again the *sūtras* of Pāṇini. Pāṇini has made the fullest use of the ellipsis for abridging his *sūtras*. He does not repeat twice a word which has the same syntactic construction in consecutive propositions. The ellipsis which is a feature of current usage for a very limited number of propositions is used by Pāṇini for a very large number of formulas. For example, in the section on the prescription of verbal affixes which come after a root, he does not repeat the mention 'after a root' in each rule, he having mentioned it at the beginning of the section once and for all, it is tacitly implied in all the rules that follow. He regularly uses this process which is called *anuvṛtti*. It is often difficult to find out a tacitly implied term because it has to be searched for very much earlier. It is a difficulty for one who has not memorised the text, for the modern researcher who works with a printed book, even when it has a word index. But the pandit who has memorised the text from a tender age has it so well in his mind that he easily retrieves each word instantaneously. Pāṇini has, in fact, elaborated his metalanguage from a syntactic mechanism, namely ellipsis, and from a mechanism of comprehension, namely that of natural memory. His formulas function not like the written formulas of the engineer, but like memorised knowledge. Similarly we can show that the composition of many Sanskrit texts is explained by the fact that they are pure knowledge to be memorised.

Another remarkable quality of the pandit is his power of concentration. His formation trains him in this. And the tradition frequently extols feats of concentration. Let us take for example what is called *aṣṭāvadhāna* 'attention to eight things'. It is a game in which the pandit is asked to pay attention to a series of eight simultaneous events but of different kinds, like a clanging of bells, a procession of persons, etc., to count them, to memorise their order of succession and to compose at the same time a Sanskrit verse on a given subject. This is within the limits of human capability, which seem to be surpassed in the case of the exercise described by the title *śatāvadhānin* 'gifted with the power of attention to one hundred things', conferred nonetheless on historical figures. Quite apart from the feat, it is true that a great part of Sanskrit literature can be understood only by a very sustained effort of concentration.

The study of Sanskrit and the handling of the *śāstras* demands more of memorisation and concentration than the everyday use of language and thought. There is a saying that a narrator of mythology (*Mahābhārata*, *Rāmāyaṇa*, *Purāṇas*) must not stop his training for a single month, the grammarian a single day, the logician a single moment.

c) *Communication and dialectic.* We have spoken of the place of the *śāstras*, grammar, exegesis and logic in the training of the pandit. This training is a *saṃskāra* which prepares him for a style of presentation of his ideas and his reasoning. For the needs of communication of ideas the pandit has not only the Sanskrit language, but a variety of powerful techniques of persuasion and defence. One of his major activities is, indeed, the intellectual exchange, which is seen as an effective means of keeping up the knowledge already acquired and enriching it. It is recommended to the pandit to remain open to all new learning and contact and inadvisable for him to stick to a single discipline: 'One must practise that [i.e. his speciality] and even more than that; all that is of quality must be learnt from others without jealousy; for the whole world is a teacher for those who are intelligent and an enemy for those who are not'. The dialogue with others or *saṃbhāṣā* —the friendly discourse (*saṃdhāya-saṃbhāṣā*) and the debate (*vigṛhya-saṃbhāṣā*)— is said to take place in an atmosphere pervaded either by friendship or by hostility. The *śāstra* of logic (*nyāya*) is largely a treatise on argumentation. It gives procedures for winning success in the debate. We note that it separates the presentation of the means of obtaining correct knowledge peculiar to scientific investigation from those of vanquishing in the debate. The sobriety of the former contrasts with the abundance of the latter. The dialectic enters into philosophy and religious controversy and at times penetrates technical disciplines and sciences such as medicine. One particular aspect, and one that can be explained by the special training of the pandit in grammar and in the exegesis of the texts, is the controversy over the interpretation of the same text. There are *Upaniṣads*, and texts such as the *Brahmasūtra*, which have been subjected to perfectly contradictory interpretations by opposing philosophical or religious schools. We must underline however the rigour and the logical value of the interpretation procedures. The procedures are regular, valid from the logical point of view and universal, common to all the interpreters. The motivations which make one resort to one or other of these procedures are specific to each school.

The underlying goal of dialectic is the maintenance of the knowledge acquired through education. It is not belittled as sterile, even though it is not accepted as a creator of truth. It forms part, however, of the intellectual life of the pandit who draws from it more than the satisfaction of displaying his talent and defeating in discussion, in that he continues in this way to exercise his faculties of presence and quickness of mind, etc. Listen to how a physician-pandit, Caraka, author of a great compilation on the medical art, which reflects the procedures and activities of the learned physicians at the beginning of the Christian era, defends the dialectic: 'A physician should debate with a physician. For a debate with an expert gives rise to that pleasure which comes from being intent on knowledge. It reinforces cleverness, it creates strength of expression, and it makes one's reputation shine forth. And if someone is confused about what they heard earlier, then because of repeated hearing it [debate] removes their uncertainty about what they heard. And for the person who is not confused about what they have heard, it reinforces their certainty even more. And it brings to his attention even those things he may not have heard before about the subject. A gracious professor teaches things gradually to a pupil who is eager to learn; out of excitement, that particular subject matter which was approved of in private may be stated all in one go by somebody who wants to win while arguing with others. That is why the wise fully approve of a debate with experts.'

d) *Poetry.* It is not poetry that defines the pandit. We have seen that it was rather the *śāstras*, grammar, etc., arts that have nothing to do with literary taste. A pandit is for this reason not a poet. And one may be poet without being pandit. However the worship of speech sharpens literary sensibility. Many pandits have been poets. It is certain that their poetry is marked, restrained, by their *saṃskāra* as pandits. It is the learned poetry of the virtuosos of the language. But the pandit's *saṃskāra* is not a superficial make-up. It is a capacity to commit the resources of the mind and language to reaching the very bottom of the reality aimed at. The great Sanskrit poetry is one of the profoundest. In it India possesses a philosophical and mystical poetry of very great richness. As between Sanskrit and Middle or Modern Indo-Aryan, there has been a wave of influence between Sanskrit poetry and the various regional poetries in both directions. Sanskrit poetry has in this way been witness to all the creation of the country in the course of history. To characterise the poetic tastes of the pandits would amount to writing the history of Indian poetry. We must indicate at least their penchant for processing everything in a poetic mould, by their recourse to verse and their concern for ornamentation and elevation. The metrical form has a mnemonic significance and always an artistic motivation. There have been examples of versified expositions of scientific and technical knowledge in all civilisations. But one must credit Sanskrit pandits with true literary masterpieces on such subjects, like the work on mathematics of Mahāvīrācārya (Karnataka, 9th century AD) in which we see a problem in arithmetic presented as follows: 'The branches of the black plum trees, lemon trees, plantain trees, areca trees, jackfruit trees, date palms, marshy date-trees, palmyra trees, nutmeg trees, mango trees and many other trees were bent under the weight of the fruits and the flowers; around lotus ponds where the bees were wandering, families of parrots and cuckoos filled the air with their diverse songs. Tired travellers arrived at the edge of this pure and refreshing wood, joyous. They were 23, they had 63 bunches of bananas, added 7 bananas and shared all equally; say the number in a bunch.'

e) *The dharma of the pandit and his responsibility.* The sense of responsibility peculiar to the pandit is defined by the idea of *dharma*. This fundamental notion of the Indian view of the world is that of a right order of things and beings. *Dharma* is universal: it includes nature, the Law and religion. It is eternal. The rules of Law and of religion were no more created by man than the laws of nature. Each thing composing the universe has its own nature which is its *dharma*. The human being has a nature distinct from the other species, a set of properties which makes him a man. His nature is defined by a form of body and a physiology, a psyche and a psychological life, a place in the human society and a social life, a place in the terrestrial and the divine universe and a relationship to maintain with the world of the beyond, etc. This nature is good in itself. Misfortune is an alteration, an attack on its integrity, by a breach in the natural course of its life at one or other level. The human being has, then, the duty of living his nature by nourishing his body, by directing his mind properly, by following the social and religious rules, etc. The awareness of this duty springs from nothing else than the awareness of the risk of unfortunate consequence in case of lapse. For, two motivations are distinguished for the actions of humans. One is the hope of acquisition of a new object and rests on desire. The other is the spontaneous feeling for following one's nature and has no other result than to leave one's nature intact. The conformity to one's nature is a duty whose accomplishment ensures being one's nature, without more. The idea of *dharma* is that of this nature of the things and of the duty to be one's nature. This duty is eternal like *dharma*. It is thus that the acts to be performed are called *nitya* 'eternal', which amounts to saying that they must be performed each time that it becomes necessary to do so according to their nature. In practice the term is used most often with regard to daily actions. It is to be noted that, from the point of view of their obligatory and natural character, no differentiation has been made between a physiological act, like nourishing the body, etc., a social custom and a religious ritual. Worship of deities is a daily duty, like eating or sleeping. And there is no gain to be expected from the accomplishment of this ritual, apart from averting the misfortune that would result from non-performance. We know that depriving oneself of food or sleep leads to an imbalance in the body, and this is the reason that has made these acts into daily duties. It is similar for the rituals.

In the consciousness of the pandit, it is the same as regards his intellectual task. The pandit is pandit with his entire being. His learning and his intellectual work are his nature. He derives from this conviction his sense of duty towards studies. This duty has the three forms which we described above: the acquisition of knowledge, the *svāḍhyāya* for the maintenance of this acquisition by recitation to himself and confrontation with other pandits, and teaching. A formula already cited by Patañjali, and frequently repeated by pandits, expresses this duty in terms of *dharma*: 'A brahmin should, without any objective, study and understand the *dharma*, i.e. the Vedas with its six ancillaries'. The six ancillaries of the Veda are the tools, such as grammar, metrics, etc. which help in using this knowledge. The expression used in this formula connotes then the knowledge of the pandit in general, i.e. Veda and *śāstras*. That implies also the Sanskrit language which is the vehicle of this knowledge and is 'Sanskrit' (*saṃskṛta*) because prepared for the accomplishment of this duty. The responsibility of the pandit appears in this way precisely to be the maintenance of the knowledge of Sanskrit. And inasmuch as Sanskrit is equated with language in itself, the pure form of speech, inasmuch as the Sanskrit texts are the source of knowledge of the universal *dharma*, the pandit is aware of having a responsibility towards the entire humanity in that regard.

f) *Orthodoxy and creativity.* Sanskrit, both a language and a culture, is a heritage that the pandit receives. He feels it is his duty to preserve it and to transmit it. Now, this heritage comprises not only a fixed knowledge, as for example the Vedic texts in their exact form, but also methods of intellectual work, an art, and hence the potential for creation. Preservation and creation are two goals pursued, and at times they conflict. The solution to this conflict, the zeal in the pursuit of either the one or the other, is a matter of personal choice. We shall mention a general trait of the pandits, valid also for other Indian intellectuals, which makes a sort of compromise between orthodoxy and the spirit of innovation. It is the fact that a creator, necessarily conscious of his originality, intentionally obscures his personality and proclaims his adherence to the ancient cultural heritage which he has received from his masters. It is a major feature of the Sanskrit literary and philosophical production that it is presented more under the form of commentaries of texts than under that of original works. Thanks to the powerful tool that the Sanskrit *śāstras* and their procedures of comprehension and of interpretation of the texts are, it was possible for a pandit to innovate even while conforming to a principle of adherence. Many of the greatest minds of India, including some of the most innovative, have resorted to the commentary to express their ideas. Śaṃkara, Rāmānuja and Madhva have each delineated a metaphysical system of great consistency and originality. These systems are perfectly irreducible to one another. They are nevertheless offered as the interpretation of the same corpus of ancient texts, namely the *Upaniṣads*, the *Brahma-sūtra* and the *Bhagavad-gītā*. And these three great thinkers do not describe themselves as creators of a system, but as interpreters of texts.

We must distinguish the orthodox pandit from the historian. The latter with his scientific mind seeks to understand the meaning of an ancient text as it might have been in the consciousness of its author and in the intellectual milieu of his epoch and will be careful not to stretch the interpretation. The orthodox pandit has no such concern for reconstruction of an ancient state. If he underlined the diachronic differences between the basic text and his period he would highlight his share of innovation and his individuality. He prefers to obscure this. For him what is important is to present as an organised whole the totality of his knowledge which contains both the ancient heritage and his new vision. The intervention of his personality is the processing of the inherited matters by the tools of the *śāstras* and his intelligence. The work of Śaṃkara is the Vedic speculative knowledge processed by the mind of a pandit fascinated by the dialectic of the 8th century and aiming at an experience of the reduction of phenomenal being to a universal principle. The work of Rāmānuja is the processing of the same Vedic learning by the mind of a pandit entirely similar as far as training in the *śāstras* is concerned, but equally strongly conditioned by the Tamil vaisnavite devotional movement of the Early Middle Ages. Their sincere orthodoxy is in their pandit-like steps for accomplishing their *dharma*, their intellectual function. The personality has in fact receded into the background before duty.

An incidental consequence of this self-effacement is that very little material has come down to the modern historian who wishes to establish the history of the Sanskrit authors. The literary history of India is a series of interrogations regarding dates and the geographical origin of authors, even and above all for the most renowned. For whereas the true facts have been overshadowed, legends have flourished. They are often interesting. They have no historical basis, but have been imagined from extant works and often give a very good description of them, being in this way more informative about the literature and the use of Sanskrit than biographical details unrelated to the works. By way of example we shall cite a legend which serves to show two types of Sanskrit pandits strongly contrasted by their zeal for orthodoxy and creation respectively. Appayya Dīkṣita, a pandit from Tamil Nadu, author of 104 works of various kinds, learned in literature as in the *śāstras*, has become renowned as the champion of orthodoxy. Jagannātha, belonging to Andhra, a very great poet, poetician and grammarian, has become renowned for his creative powers. They lived at the end of the sixteenth century and the beginning of the seventeenth. They were powerful intellects and indefatigable dialecticians, and their works are opposed to each other in particular on points of poetics. The legend says that Jagannātha, on completing his studies under great masters in his native province in the South, set out for the North in search of fame and wealth. He reached Delhi, presented himself before the Great Moghul, but could not win his favour. He was received coldly and sent away with a trifling gift. While leaving the assembly hall he muttered under his breath the beginning of a line of verse about the meagre present 'Barely enough for salt...'. Courtesans who heard him reported these words to the Emperor. Jagannātha was summoned back and ordered to repeat what he had said. Extemporarily he repeated the same words and completed the verse so as to transform it into a compliment: 'Barely enough for salt are the presents of others / The Emperor of Delhi, and God, alone know how to reward.' His presence of mind was appreciated. The pandit was rewarded and appointed to the court. He became the favourite partner of the Emperor in the game of chess. One day the Emperor was close to winning. He asked the pandit to express a wish; he would grant it, whatever it might be, if the pandit won. At the same instant, a Moghul princess came into the room. Jagannātha was troubled by her beauty. He asked for her hand as the prize of the game and set his heart on winning. The Emperor was obliged to give the Muslim princess to the brahmin. The couple lived happily. When old age came, Jagannātha desired to spend his retirement in the holy city of Vārāṇasī. He arrived there, taking also with him his Muslim wife with whom he was still very much in love. This misalliance was not to the liking of the brahmins of that sacred town. He aroused above all the indignation of Appayya Dīkṣita who, having come on a pilgrimage from the extreme South of the country, saw him one day lying on the bank of the sacred river with the princess in his arms. A corner of the princess's scarf covered his face, leaving only a tuft of gray hair visible. The worthy and virtuous Dīkṣita, without having recognised him, expressed his indignation and his pity on seeing an old man so forgetful of his last duties of piety, beginning with these words: 'How, at the end of your life, with death approaching, do you remain lying...'. Jagannātha interrupted him and completed the verse himself: 'or sleep comfortably, the Gaṅgā watching by your side'.

The insolence of such a reply turned everyone away from him. It is said that even the Gaṅgā, the river that purifies men of all sins, receded before him when he went down the steps to bathe in her. Having reached the last step, he began to compose a hymn to the divine river. At each verse the Gaṅgā rose a step. At the last verse she carried him off into her waters with the princess he so much loved. This hymn, the *Gaṅgā-laharī* 'the wave of the Gaṅgā', is a short masterpiece of great melodious charm, and condenses all of India's sublime thoughts, all the love nurtured by her for her great river in the centuries that have gone by. The adventure, the misalliance and the disregard for orthodoxy did not prevent Jagannātha from being recognised as *paṇḍita-rāja* 'king of pandits'. He is one of the great Sanskrit poets. And he was able to create a renaissance in the one thousand year old science of poetics (*alaṃkāra-śāstra*).

CHAPTER IV

THE USES OF SANSKRIT

I. Spoken language

It is as difficult to describe the use of Sanskrit as a spoken language as to determine who, other than the pandits, spoke Sanskrit. Too few documents on this aspect of Sanskrit have come down to us. As, by contrast, the attestations of scholarly and artificial use are plentiful, some have gone so far as to doubt the existence of a spoken Sanskrit. In reality what one finds difficult to pinpoint is the Sanskrit spoken by speakers other than pandits. But there is every reason to suppose that it was used by the pandits for the needs of everyday communication among themselves and in their circles. There exist also indications of the use of Sanskrit in a wider circle, that of pandits in an unlearned family circle, in princely courts, in certain cultivated milieus, and in every good society even non-brahmin and non-noble. There are indications that Sanskrit was, to some extent, accessible to people as a whole. The *Nāṭya-śāstra*, a great treatise on dramaturgy, of uncertain date but at least earlier than the sixth century AD, recommends for the theatre a language 'devoid of obscure words and meanings, which is easily appreciated by the common people'; it employs the term *janapada* which is used for the popular strata of the society. The *Kāmasūtra*, whose date is also uncertain, while describing the social life of fashionable society, advises against speaking too much Sanskrit or too much in the local language. The poetician Bhāmaha (eighth century AD) speaks of clarity of language in Sanskrit poetry, in other words 'poetry whose meaning is understood by all, from scholars to women and children'. There is therefore a possibility of an unlearned audience and consequently a spoken Sanskrit. On the other hand we have already emphasised that Sanskrit readily assimilated new words and usages drawn from local tongues which existed alongside it, everywhere and in every period. Assimilating the language to some extent to the prevailing local language made it more accessible. The noticeable intrusion of roots and other grammatical elements, words and turns of phrase into Sanskrit in every age indicates clearly that it has been used for communication with people other than pandits. It must not be doubted that Sanskrit has really been a spoken language.

We know something of its spoken form by what we can infer from the works of the grammarians and from the scholarly literature in which it does figure occasionally. In the works of grammarians we find words that escape all their ingenuity for analysis and that cannot be accommodated under any of their rules. Pāṇini offers a number of exceptional forms as ready-made. They are so many attestations of natural idiomatic forms. For his part Patañjali adds many popular forms and draws attention to the case of forms which can be deduced from the rules, but which he does not know to be in usage. For example the rule constructs perfect tense forms for all the three persons in all the three numbers. Now, Patañjali remarks that the regularly formed second plural of certain verbs: *ūṣa*, *tera*, *cakra*, *peca* 'you have resided, crossed, made, cooked' are no longer in use, and that the constructions [*yūyam*] *uṣitāḥ*, *tīrṇāḥ*, *kṛtavantaḥ*, and *pakvavantaḥ* are used in their place. He does not conclude from this that the rules are wrong. He deduces that he does not know all the usages and that they can exist elsewhere than in the milieu that he knows. 'I am in this world', he says, 'I am not the world'. This reveals his conception and his usage of the language, and at the same time suggests a demarcation between spoken language and scholarly language. The spoken usage of a group, like that of Patañjali, has its limitations of which only the members of the group are aware, for example this limitation on the use of the perfect in all grammatical persons except one. The scholarly language is based on the rules and does not take note of such limitations on usage. Patañjali knows the local usage, which testifies that he was using a spoken Sanskrit. But he also sees Sanskrit as universal, as being in use beyond his personal experience. It is the scholarly Sanskrit, obtained by a sort of generalization of the spoken language, which leads to the increased validness of its structures.

Literature also reveals these two levels of the language both of which are widely represented. Two styles can clearly be distinguished: the descriptive and the spoken. In Sanskrit drama they are clearly separated. There is the dialogue in prose and there are the lyrical digressions in verse. The latter sometimes assume too much importance and stifle the living dialogue. But in a work in which the two styles are well balanced, we have a good many examples of spoken Sanskrit. The play *Mṛcchakaṭikā* 'The little clay cart' of Śūdraka offers one of the best examples of this. We encounter this contrast of style in poetry and in the very original genre of the

Sanskrit novel (*kathā*, *ākhyāyikā*). The latter genre, whose model is the *Kādambarī* of Bāṇa Bhaṭṭa, borders on the novel in that its purpose is the narration of a story, and pure poetry in that the description overrides the narration. The descriptions run into long sentences, each often longer than a page, of surprisingly simple syntax, but of complex literary structure, exercising all the conventions and ornamentations of Sanskrit poetics. Every now and again a dialogue with brief, simple sentences not devoid of elegance is introduced; it is a breath of fresh air, a breath of life, a return to earth, after the dense style of the sublime descriptions which are pure products of the poetic imagination. The striking contrast between the two styles reveals to us clearly that there is here an intentional effort by the author to reproduce an element of natural life. And that is without any doubt a true attestation of spoken language. The contrast is less striking in other works where the poetic style is not so laboured, for example in the great epics of *Rāmāyaṇa* and *Mahābhārata*. But the two styles can still be recognised in them. In scholarly poetry, there exists a game which consists of introducing living dialogue into the constraining metre of a stanza, which restricts the choice to the briefest possible replies. After all is said and done, it can be said that spoken Sanskrit is present everywhere and well documented in the literature. But it has to be searched for amidst scholarly Sanskrit. This situation reflects reality, the fact that the pandit uses the language at two levels.

II. Language of communication

The oldest Vedic quickly expanded beyond its earliest geographical limits. This expansion in space brought it into contact with various local languages. One imagines easily that it could from then on serve as a lingua franca between regions differing in language. By the time of Patañjali it had spread across the whole of the Indo-Gangetic plain. It must have played this role, over this vast area, at least in the circles of learned brahmins. It is in fact only after the Christian era that a generalised role as a language of ordinary communication is clearly attested for it. Our best evidence on this point is epigraphy.

We have seen that epigraphy is Middle Indian in its early stages. Aśoka published his ideas of peace and tolerance in the four corners of his vast empire in an unstandardised Middle Indian. Prakrit epigraphy developed considerably until the Christian era and in the first three centuries of it, notably under the Kuṣāṇas. In the region of Mathurā there appears a Prakrit heavily mingled with Sanskrit. It is used in inscriptions which are mostly Buddhist or Jaina. The first inscription of importance that is purely Sanskrit which has come down to us issues from the kṣatrapa king Rudradāman (150 BC). It is the first dated example of the ornamental descriptive style of classical Sanskrit poetry and the first attestation of the use of Sanskrit for official purposes in a royal court. The level of perfection already reached implies earlier productions, of which no trace has remained. It would be an exaggeration to take this inscription as an absolute starting point. It bears witness to the rising use of Sanskrit which will, progressively and after several centuries, replace Prakrit in the epigraphy in all of India and will maintain itself down to a period very close to ours.

The contents of these inscriptions are most often the recording of an act of piety, of charity, of public utility: gifts of lands to brahmins, to a nobleman as a reward for his services, the foundation of temples, schools, the construction of irrigation reservoirs, various administrative measures. The panegyric of the reigning king, with the history of his dynasty, or the eulogy of the founder serve generally as an introduction to the description of the act. In the south whose languages are Dravidian the panegyric is frequently in Sanskrit and the act in the local language. Since it was essential that the act concerning the inhabitants of the place should be read and understood by all, the use of their language was preferable for that. As for the panegyric, the history of the king, it was probably already known to the subjects. It was interesting to make it known outside the kingdom. Now, Sanskrit was the most stabilised language, which had replaced the Prakrits which were never standardised, and had become the only language common to the entire sub-continent. It compelled recognition as the language of royal propaganda. In the consciousness of the authors of the title-deeds Sanskrit was the universal and eternal language. Publishing the acts and the history of a king in this language would further their diffusion and their remembrance.

Sanskrit has been used in the same way outside the borders of India. In the Hinduised kingdoms of south east Asia, the monarchs, especially the builders of the monuments of Kampuchea (Cambodia), have very closely imitated their Indian counterparts, by having their history written in Sanskrit poetry of a very high level. The presence of a large number of Sanskrit inscriptions extending as far away as Borneo and issuing from royal courts points to the fact that Sanskrit was a language of international diplomacy.

Sanskrit must also have served as a language of communication between various regions and various nations for other purposes such as travel, trade, etc. On this use, while there is a paucity of direct documentation, there are nevertheless some indications. The Chinese pilgrim Yi-tsing (635-713) who set out for India by sea in 671 made a long stopover at Śrīvijaya (Palembang in the island of Sumatra). He learnt spoken Sanskrit there, arrived in India at Tamralipti in Bengal in 673 and was able from his arrival to use the language. He found it to be useful for his travels as well as his research. He visited the places sacred to Buddhism, made a long stay at Nālandā, returned to China in around 685, carrying with him a large number of Sanskrit texts, and devoted the rest of his life to translating them into Chinese. Thus we observe that Sanskrit was the language of travellers. While this appears to be quite natural inside India, it is interesting to see that Sanskrit could be learnt in the seventh century in Sumatra. And this indicates that it was internationally used for practical purposes.

III. Scientific and technical language

The earliest scientific texts composed in India belong to the Vedic corpus. The users of the Vedas, as we have seen, created six ancillary disciplines (*vedāṅga*) aiming at codifying their use of the language and their practice of religious rituals. Four among them concern the language: grammar (*vyākaraṇa*), metrics (*chandas*), phonetics (*śikṣā*), vocabulary (*nighaṇṭu*). The last two are concerned with religious activity: ceremonial (*kalpa*) and astronomy (*jyotiṣa*). For each, manuals have been compiled. In the area of the ceremonial there is a section which describes the solemn sacrifices, some of which involve the construction of a brick altar of a special shape. This section, called *śulba*, makes use of practical geometrical constructions. In the formularies (*śulba-sūtra*) of several Vedic schools, we find a general chapter which is an abstract and systematic exposition of geometry, perhaps the oldest coherent and substantial treatises in the history of mathematics (their date cannot unfortunately be determined with any accuracy, even to within a century). The method of research and exposition compares very well with that of the grammarians: general rules inferred from empirical and experimental observations, a tendency to write in formulas, a practical arrangement of rules into sequences of application, etc. The Vedic period possessed true astronomical knowledge, but the text on astronomy entitled *Jyotiṣa-vedāṅga* which has come down to us is of disputed date and we do not have it perhaps in its original form. So mathematical formulas were the starting point of scientific exposition in India.

The sciences have known a remarkable and unbroken development in this country throughout its history. Born in the circle of Sanskrit men of letters, and developed at the same time as grammar, they always retained this association with pandits. Sanskrit remained the quasi-exclusive medium of scientific expression until the Moghul period. The processes of thought, reflection and research were conducted with the intellectual tools of the Sanskrit *śāstras*. Sanskrit owes this function to the historical fact that mathematical reflection was born in the circle of Vedic ritual specialists. It owes it also to its character as a language that can be adapted to every new use and to the codification of the procedures of expression and of interpretation made by the pandits, which make it an instrument better suited to systematic and logical thought. Sanskrit had received the saṃskāra, or in other words a remarkable preparation for being used for intellectual work, and as a consequence was the preferred language for scientific work.

From this point of view it can be said that Sanskrit has served the development of the sciences. What has been said of the sciences is also true for the technical disciplines. And one can say that in India was found expressed in Sanskrit all that the human spirit could attempt in the field of sciences and technical disciplines in the course of ancient and medieval history.

Conversely this monopoly in the expression of scientific and technical knowledge has served the development, the generalised use and the expansion of Sanskrit. Scientific interest and technical need led to the learning and the use of this language, even in circles other than those of brahmins and in professions other than religious and literary. Here again we see that Sanskrit is not just the religious language of restricted circles of brahmins, as is imagined too often. It is first of all a utilitarian language, the vehicle of all categories of knowledge, at the service of the users of knowledge irrespective of their origin.

IV. Literary language

Sanskrit does not have the monopoly of poetic and literary expression in India. In every period it had to face competition from local languages, both Indo-Aryan and Dravidian. Productions of aesthetic value are numerous in Sanskrit. They are quite as much in the other languages. The literary developments took place simultaneously. And at the same time two forces were at play: on the one hand processes of development taking place within each literature independently, on the other a number of possibilities of mutual influence. Sanskrit literature is comprehended through the study of its original structures, of the forms with which it had endowed itself in conformity with its goals, as also by the study of its borrowings and its influence on other languages, of its reactions to the outside movements to which it was witness and of the reactions of the literatures with which it was in contact. It was not necessarily always accepted as a model. It had to face up to regionalist sentiments and reactions of rejection. In this respect Sanskrit is no longer the dominant language, no longer the only source. There is a literary phenomenon which is Indian, not that of Sanskrit alone. India is the preferred ground for comparative literature, an area of research which is as yet unexplored. The most striking example is that of the epic cycle of the *Rāmāyaṇa*, the only one that modern research has begun to take up. This epic, first attested in Sanskrit, is the work of Vālmīki, and is one of the great monuments of universal literature. But it is appropriated by almost all the great regional literatures of India and south east Asia, often with a great originality. And each of these literatures claims its *Rāmāyaṇa* as its masterpiece and as the primary locus of its individuality.

In the Sanskrit tradition the *Rāmāyaṇa* of Vālmīki is said to be the first *kāvya*. The pandits see in it their source and their principal model. In their consciousness the term *kāvya* captures the essence of the idea of literary quality. To translate this word by 'poetry' is to restrict too narrowly its scope. It is said to have two aspects, *dṛśya* 'for the eyes', which refers to the theatre, and *śravya* 'for the ear' which refers to all other literary forms. Etymologically *kāvya* is the work of a *kavi*, an old Vedic name for the author of hymns, for the inspired sage, for the possessor of speech that is effectual in prayer and in sacrifice. The *kavi* is not only an author of text, but also its enunciator. The liturgic word is vocalised aloud, the resonance of the voice and the diction having an essential role in the success of the sacrifice. The *kavi* is the author of this act of speech. The classical *kāvya* has always retained something of this ancient value. It is an act of speech with an emotional and aesthetic aim, intended for auditory communication, in which the sound has as much role as the sense. The idea of written representation and communication by reading is absent. The Sanskrit *kāvya* is not the art of letters but the art of spoken words. It exploits all the resources of the language. The Sanskrit poet builds on the structures which he is aware of as a pandit, in other words on the procedures of construction and comprehension laid down by the *śāstras*. His raw material is made up of the basic elements: the phonemes, and the minimal morphemes such as roots and suffixes. One often has the feeling that he is constructing words more than he does sentences, than he does discourse. His work can only be understood well if on the one hand one is attentive to the Paninian etymology of his words, and on the other if one has recourse to the interpretational procedures of the *śāstras*, among which figures the art of poetic ornaments which owes much to the *vyākaraṇa*.

The effects of this attitude on the language are many and complex. Never perhaps has the language been so much worked on as by Sanskrit poets. The major features of the language of the classical *kāvya*, of which representative works have appeared from the Christian era to our day, are the elimination of syntax, the creation of new words, the systematisation of synonymy and the pursuit of homonymy. The syntactical relationships ordinarily expressed in Sanskrit by case endings are rendered implicit by recourse to word-compounding. The sentence has a tendency to get reduced to one or two terms qualified by a series of qualifiers which are long compounds. Each of the latter is as it were the equivalent of a complete subordinate clause; for the long compound is seen as a transformation of a group of inflected words into a new unit in which the case endings that are tools for the expression of syntactical relationships are eliminated, in which the entire syntax is only implicit. The effect of this removal of the morpheme-tools, leaving only the sequence of noun stems, is an extreme density. That defies all translation into an analytical language and puts to the test the mental faculties of the hearer who must reconstitute the major part which is implicit. We shall cite as an example a compound of Bāṇa Bhaṭṭa (early seventh century) describing pomegranate seeds given to a parrot: *Hari-nakhara-bhinna-matta-mātaṅga-kumbha-mukta-rakta-ārdra-muktāphala-tviṃṣi dāḍima-bījāni* which is the sequence of the words 'lion-claw-broken-intoxicated-elephant-hump-shed-blood-damp-pearl-sparkle pomegranate-seeds'. The Sanskrit compound is understood from right to left. The knowledge of the structure of compounds, as they are described by Pāṇini, lets the hearer understand: 'pomegranate seeds whose sparkle is like that of pearls moistened by blood shed from the hump of intoxicated elephants torn by the claws of a lion' (The Indian elephant has two frontal humps which are said by poetic convention to contain pearls).

The Sanskrit poet takes the liberty of creating new words, following the construction procedures of the grammars, ignoring all limitation imposed by usage: compound words, secondary derivatives, but also primary derivatives, which shows clearly that his art is focussed on elementary morphemes. We see emerge in the *kāvya* a characteristic profusion of root-nouns, like *tviṣ* in the example above.

The natural use of a language seeks to separate synonyms, by establishing differentiating nuances, by allocating their use to separate registers: female, woman, lady, etc. are employed each in their own context and are not interchangeable. The instances of absolute synonymy are in fact very rare. The Sanskrit *kāvya* contravenes this tendency. We note its proclivity to do away with nuances and its unfettered use of synonyms in all contexts. One finds in this way more easily the word that will fit in a constraining metrical schema. That serves also the pursuit of alliterations and sound. The most remarkable is the creation of homonyms and of sequences with double meaning. The *kāvya* affects expressions of double entendre (*śleṣa*, literally amalgam). There are in Sanskrit simple words with multiple meanings, they are simple homonyms. The poets give themselves the liberty of creating complex homonyms by combining with each other simple words, initially different. A typical game of the *kāvya* is to establish a comparison between two terms with the aid of such a sequence with double meaning. For example Bāṇa Bhaṭṭa compares a family of brahmins to the flood of the Gaṅgā by saying that the two are *sakalakalāgamagambhīra*, a sequence which represents the words *sakala-kalā-āgama-gambhīra* which describes the family as being 'profoundly learned in all the arts and traditions'; or else: *sa-kalakala-āgama-gambhīra* which describes the flood of the river descended from the sky as being 'profound in its fall accompanied by tumult'. The comparison is established solely by the fact that the respective properties of the two terms, although different, are expressed by the same sequence of sounds.

V. Religious language

We must discern two uses of the language in the context of religion. On one side it is a simple vehicle of information on religion. On another side it has an additional value as the word revealed by God or the word of a saint, and is endowed with a power and used as such in rituals. The first type of use brings nothing new to Sanskrit, apart from the fact that it makes it the language of a voluminous literature of mythological texts (*purāṇas*, etc.), of technical texts of rituals (*tantras*), of devotional texts, etc. The second type of use gives Sanskrit a new dimension. It makes it the eternal language of the revealed texts and of *mantras* or formulas endowed with a power.

Sanskrit is well-known as religious language. There is too much of a tendency to think of it as being nothing but that, which is very inaccurate, for we have seen that it has many other uses and the only one in which it overshadows all the other languages, one in which it has practically a monopoly, is that of scientific and technical language. It is not, indeed, the sole religious language of India. It is that of the old Vedic religion. But in the context of Hinduism it has for certain functions to come to terms with the great regional devotional literatures. Pāli is the language of Theravāda Buddhism in Śrīlaṅkā and in south east Asia. Sanskrit is the language of Mahāyāna Buddhism and is used in liturgy only in the tantric schools. In Jainism it is even less in evidence. The Jaina canon is in Ārdhamāgadhī and Sanskrit is neither the liturgical language, nor the revealed language, but only that of information. And even this role it has to share with other Prakrits such as Mahārāṣṭrī Jaina, etc. and modern languages like Gujarātī, Kannaḍa, etc.

1. Language of the religious sources

We have seen above how the Veda always received from a master is conceived of as being without beginning, uncreated and eternal, Sanskrit participating in the eternity of the text of which it is the medium. Furthermore the eternal Veda is a source par excellence of all information on religious duties, the means of knowing *dharma*. There is the natural aspect of *dharma* which one knows spontaneously, like the necessities of life and moral obligations, but as far as rituals are concerned there is no source other than the Vedas. Sanskrit is the depository of a knowledge which one would not possess without it.

The *Tantras* are the manuals of the practitioners of the shaivite, vaishnavite, etc. religions which constitute Hinduism. These texts are also considered as being without human authors. Their origin is God, namely Śiva, Viṣṇu, or more precisely the universal consciousness which is the essence of God. This consciousness is said to activate itself and descend on earth according to a well-defined process of transmission. It takes a body whose substance is a higher form of speech. It is then uttered by a manifested form of God. This hypostasis transmits it to another divinity and by transmission through a succession of beings of decreasing quality the primordial consciousness of God becomes the knowledge on religion in the form of the Sanskrit text which is pronounced by a human master.

2. The concept of *mantra*

The use of Sanskrit in liturgy makes it sacred. The basic idea is that of a supernatural power belonging to the spoken word. It seems that this power is conceived of above all else for the act of speech, the formula vocalised in the course of the ritual, but not for the language as such. Or if one speaks of a sacred character, of a power of language, it is by transference, because it is the language of the formula. The latter is designated by the term *mantra*. The word is etymologically derived from the root *man* 'to think'. Indian grammarians see in it a derivative of a specialised root *matr*[i] for which they recognise the meaning of hidden speech. This etymology highlights the secluded character of the ritual formulas. Another etymology emanating from tantric texts makes it a derivative of two roots: *man* 'to think' and *trai* 'to protect'. The two characteristics indicated by this analysis are the spiritual nature and its value as a means to salvation. The *mantra* can be extracted from the Veda or be constructed from rules taught in the *Tantras*. It participates then in the eternity of the first and the divine origin of the second. The construction of *mantras* is, moreover, an elaborate art and constitutes such an important part of Tantrism that it is made into a discipline in its own right called *mantra-śāstra*. These features differentiate then the *mantra* from the formula of common use. A number of explanations for this difference have been considered. We shall cite as an example a remarkable Tantric conception. In the *Śaiva-siddhānta* school the *mantra* is seen as a spiritual being situated at the highest point of the theological scale. It is a soul liberated from the world of transmigration, whose power of consciousness is universal, is equal to that of Śiva, but which remains inferior to the supreme Śiva, because He gives it the responsibility of distributing His grace to the souls still in bondage. For carrying out his mission, this messenger of divine grace takes a body whose substance is speech. This speech is seen as having four forms: a transcendental form (*parā*) evolved into a subtle form (*paśyantī*) accessible only to yogins, then into a form called *madhyamā* which is human mental speech and lastly a form called *vaikharī* which is the audible form used by the performers of rituals. Recall that the pure consciousness of the soul is seen as an omniscient and omnipotent power (*śakti*). The nature of liberated soul attributed to the *mantra* accounts for its effectual power in the ritual. Its nature as God's representative accounts for its role in salvation.

The idea that the *mantra* is Sanskrit and that there are no *mantras* in other languages is widespread. In the context of Hinduism this idea does not seem to have been shaken. It is true that regional languages claim a sacred status and that devotional texts are introduced in the course of the ritual. It remains true nonetheless that an effectual power is considered as the distinguishing quality of Sanskrit. For example among the vaishnavaites of Tamil Nadu called Śrīvaiṣṇavas, the Tamil devotional hymns addressed to Viṣṇu composed by the Ālwārs are said to be a Dravidian Veda and they are recited as part of the ritual, alternately with recitations of the Sanskrit *Yajurveda*, at the time of the ritual worship of Viṣṇu or processions of icons of this god. There are elaborate rituals whose goal is to accomplish the presence of the divinity with its true essence in the place of worship and in the icon that is the subject of the material worship. Only the power of *mantras* is considered as having the ability to accomplish this presence. To our knowledge this fundamental ritual is ensured by the Sanskrit *mantras*. The texts in other languages, introduced into Hindu rituals, seem to concern above all the expression of devotional sentiments, as desired by devotees. And it is natural that the population of devotees, among whom the Sanskrit pandits are only a small minority, should be able to express its love of God in its own language. Sanskrit has then in exclusivity the transcendental power and remains the technical instrument of the rite of accomplishment of the presence and of the action of God. As regards the participation and expression of their sentiments by the Faithful, it is shared between Sanskrit and their own languages.

CHAPTER V

THE EXPANSION OF SANSKRIT

From its cradle in the north-west of the Indian sub-continent, in the course of a life of perhaps four millennia, Sanskrit has spread through all of Asia to the east of Iran. The forms under which it has been used are diverse. We must describe this expansion by specifying the dates and the geographical areas, the forms of use and the users. These different factors of the phenomenon of its expansion can only be determined reliably if there are direct documents concerning them. The texts are not enough; or at any rate they are indirect documents; one cannot draw inferences from them about users, etc. The ancient period is, as we saw, the subject of conjectures, because in this period it is only documented by the texts whose chronology is itself very hypothetical. After the Christian era more conclusive documents are available to historians. These are the mediaeval inscriptions of the various kingdoms of South India which relate the creation of brahmin settlements and the founding of Sanskrit schools; the epigraphical data of south-east Asia which, better than a text or an influence that could always come from elsewhere, attest by their presence the use of Sanskrit in that area; and finally the travel accounts of men of letters in India, in Central Asia, in China, etc.

I. The expansion in India

We know from Patañjali that Sanskrit could be used in all of the Indo-Gangetic plain. The expansion in the rest of India is a phenomenon later than the Christian era. The epigraphical data show that Sanskrit becomes the preferred language of the panegyrics and of the royal acts in the Gupta empire (third to fifth century AD). The kingdoms which are founded in the South after this period, Kadamba, Cāḷukya, Pallava, etc. increasingly make use of Sanskrit. And one can say that from the seventh century Sanskrit has played the role of a language of diplomacy over the entire territory of India. The interest in Vedic culture, existing from the beginnings of the Christian era, developed considerably in the South from the same period. Epigraphy relates a number of endowments of land to brahmins. The object of a brahmin settlement is not directly to spread the Sanskrit language. In the mind of the donors it is first the idea of spreading *dharma*, the right order of the world. The king who is mindful of the good order of his territory decides the settlement of representatives of the first class (*varṇa*) of the ideal society, since *dharma* requires the presence of the four classes. But among the brahmins there were men of letters specialised in the recitation, teaching and exposition of the Vedas which are the source of *dharma*. Among the pandits there were also specialists in Sanskrit treatises, which are repositories of scientific and technical knowledge. There were finally specialists of Sanskrit and of the *śāstras*, studied and taught for their own sake. The establishment of Sanskrit and Vedic colleges frequently accompanies these endowments. The sense of conformity to *dharma*, requiring every kind of learning, religious, philosophical, juridical, scientific, technical, etc., has created the need for Sanskrit and has served its expansion. The agent of this expansion is the person of the pandit. He is so well implanted in the South from the 7th-8th century that the South begins to produce great pandits in Sanskrit. The contribution of the South to Sanskrit literature in all fields will from then on be fundamental. The founders of the three major trends of Sanskrit philosophy are Śaṃkara (8th century), Rāmānuja (1017-1137?) and Madhva (1238-1317), all three from the extreme south of the peninsula. The greatest enterprise of commentary of the whole of Vedic literature, on which, even today, the comprehension of the Veda depends, is that which was directed by Sāyaṇa thanks to the patronage of the emperors of Vijayanagar (Karnataka) in the fourteenth century.

That Sanskrit suffered from the Muslim rule in the north of India is a controversial issue. While a centre may have declined on occasion, another prospered in the same period and in a region not far away. What is remarkable is that continuity has been ensured as regards the preservation and development of the Sanskritic learning in the whole of India, despite political, economic, social and religious upheavals which may have occurred in the course of mediaeval history.

The millennium which stretches from the 7th to the 17th century is the great era of Sanskrit and of the pandits. Sanskrit appears in this period in all the fields of use that one has been able to acknowledge for it, and it secures its predominance in some of them, as a pan-Indian language of communication and of scientific language. The pandit has never been so close to the governing power, either because he participates in the administration or because he receives its patronage, has never played so many different roles in the intellectual life, nor exercised so much influence on language and culture. During this period, the pandits have probably been the foremost creators and promoters of India's rich civilisation.

II. The expansion outside India

It is attested by the presence of Sanskrit texts, preserved or translated, and by the existence of inscriptions in regions far removed from India. Now, no document testifies to any substantial Indian emigration, or to any external conquests leading to a political domination or to settlements of population, or any form of lasting colonisation. One can imagine neither a colonisation by a population for whom Sanskrit was the principal language, nor an imposition of Sanskrit by Indian monarchs exercising their power in some manner or other. The expansion of Sanskrit can only be the work of pandits. The travels of men of letters beyond the borders of India are remembered.

From the beginning of the Christian era Buddhist ideas penetrated China. This propagation was supported by an immense work of research and translation of Sanskrit texts. Indian pandits and Chinese men of letters have taken part in it. A celebrated example is that of Kumārajīva (344-413). He belonged to an Indian family which traditionally held the office of minister. However his father by religious inclination had given up this office, then left his country, crossed the Pamir and reached the kingdom of Kucha in Central Asia. He became the chaplain and the son-in-law of the king of this land. Kumārajīva was his first son. Taken by his mother to Kashmir, this remarkably gifted child received from a celebrated master, Bandhudatta, his education in Buddhist literature and began to win fame in debate. Then he returned with his mother to Kucha, but was intercepted by the king of Kashgar. The sequel to his story was one of travels in all of central Asia, and of an unceasing activity of study and propaganda, until the day when a Chinese general Lu Kuang, having taken Kucha, took him to his capital Leang-cheu. Finally Kumārajīva was taken to the court of the later Ts'ins at Ch'ang-an, a great centre of Chinese culture in the north. We owe to him the supervision of a considerable work of translation of Sanskrit works, the task being entrusted to Chinese men of letters who had learnt Sanskrit, as well as to polyglot Indians. Learned and educated Chinese have distinguished themselves by their travels of piety and study to the places sacred to Buddhism, and by their work of translation. The most famous among them is Hiuan-tsang (602-664).

Buddhism similarly spread into Tibet, especially from the seventh century, thanks to the initiative of the king Sroṅ-bcan-sgam-po and to the decisive mission of the grammarian Thonmi Saṃbhoṭa to India. The Tibetan men of letters not only learnt Sanskrit and acquired a great knowledge of Sanskrit Buddhist texts, but borrowed the Indian script and elaborated a literary form of their language for the needs of translation from Sanskrit.

The major part of the vast Sanskrit Buddhist literature has been lost in India. It is known to us only through the Chinese and Tibetan translations. It is possible to reconstruct an original Sanskrit text, particularly from the Tibetan versions because of the literal nature and regularity of their style of translation, the Chinese translations being found to be more free.

These translations testify to the knowledge of Sanskrit by men of letters who do not belong to India, and this is attested in central Asia and in China. An even more remarkable fact is the production of Sanskrit works outside India. This is attested especially in south east Asia, under the form of inscriptions which are spread over the period from the 5th to the 15th century. The largest number were composed and inscribed in Kampuchea (Cambodia). They concern generally royal acts relating to religious endowments, containing a panegyric of the king in verse, in a very ornamented *kāvya* style, then a text in Khmer prose. There is sometimes a eulogy of the chaplain (*purohita*) of the king. In some cases we are told that it is a scholarly brahmin coming from India, like Śrīnivāsa Kavi, *ācārya* of the king Jayavarman III 'who, although born in his glorious country, excellent connoisseur of the Veda, has come here for purifying the beautiful regions of Kambu (Kampuchea)'. It must also be the case of Śivasoma, *ācārya* of Indravarman I (877-889), who received from the monarch a parasol, the royal insignia par excellence, and who is extolled as student of Bhagavat Śaṃkara who, according to G. Coedès, is none other than the great Indian philosopher. We see by this document that pandits came from India to Kampuchea, on the invitation of the kings of this country who needed them for a purificatory purpose, in other words for executing the rites of *dharma* which must ensure the good of the king and of the kingdom.

There are many similar references to Indian masters honoured by the kings of Kampuchea, and appointed to the government. They were able to carry on their intellectual activities there, establish a tradition, teach and above all give their directives and advice to Kampuchean artists and intellectuals. They are perhaps not the sole authors of the inscriptions. They are not the builders of the monuments, neither are they their direct and only inspiration. Those monuments are not Indian, nor of a purely Indian religion; there is a Khmer conception of the mountain temple, and a step pyramid style that is Khmer. But there is certainly an Indian teaching at the beginning. A few pandits were perhaps enough to provide the basic impetus for the construction of the largest monumental and artistic complex of humanity.

CONCLUSION

Sanskrit is still a living language today, because there are still pandits who choose to live the ideal of their ancestors. But Sanskrit and they themselves have suffered very serious onslaughts in modern times. From the 16th century the great Neo-Indian languages assert themselves with literary movements that carry great popular support. Sanskrit was not hindered by them in its own development; it assisted them in theirs by providing them with vocabulary, etc. But this role of being a source relegated it to the background. The Muslim rule from the 17th century deprived Sanskrit of two of its monopolies, that of language of communication and diplomacy, and that of vehicle of scientific and technical knowledge. For it is Persian which, at the peak of the Moghul empire, replaced it, as the language of domestic and external relations. The Europeans who came for purposes of trade and who were then settling down slowly in the country, learnt Persian. Sanskrit pandits were still serving in the administration controlled by the Muslim sovereigns, but they had to add Persian to their learning and use it more and more. They compiled a Persian grammar on the model of that of Pāṇini. The *Upaniṣads* and other fundamental Sanskrit texts were translated into this language. In the scientific field Persian and Arabic were in keen competition with Sanskrit. For this period it is calculated that 400 manuscripts of mathematical works in Arabic and Persian were produced in India, as against 120 in Sanskrit. There is however no deterioration in the major traditional uses of Sanskrit, no interruption either in its teaching, or in the development of the *śāstras*, or in its literary creation, or in its religious use. It is a period of blossoming and revival in the studies of grammar (*vyākaraṇa*) and logic (*navya-nyāya*).

European colonisation struck an even more severe blow. In the beginning of the 19th century it replaced Persian by English as the language of communication and Administration; it put an end to the development of scientific and technical studies, so much so that English remained the sole vehicle of this knowledge; it had delusions of superiority over the culture of India; and while it made some endowments for the protection of Sanskrit, this was not without a scornful look for what the French naturalist Jacquemont, travelling in India and much too close to the English colonial circles, called 'the picturesque ruin whose fall the Government is trying to delay by its liberality'.

Sanskrit was brought to the attention of the West by the researches of some pioneers in the seventeenth and the eighteenth centuries: the Sanskrit grammar compiled about 1660 by the German Jesuit Heinrich Roth (Dillingen 1620-Agra 1668), that of the French Jesuit Jean-François Pons (Rodez 1688-1752?) which was sent to France in 1732, the English translation of the *Bhagavad-Gītā* in 1786 by the Englishman Charles Wilkins. Then the Latin translation of a Persian version of the *Upaniṣads* in 1801 by the Frenchman Anquetil-Duperron (1731-1805) revealed the philosophy of India. The German Franz Bopp (Mainz 1791-Berlin 1867) founded the study of the comparative grammar of the Indo-European languages. The Frenchman Eugène Bournouf (Paris 1801-id.1852) founded the scientific study of Indian Buddhism from the Sanskrit and Pāli sources, and that of Hinduism from Sanskrit texts. The German Max Müller (Dessau 1823-Oxford 1900) published the first printed edition of the *Ṛgveda* (Oxford 1849-1875).

In India itself the traditions of Sanskrit study were not interrupted during the colonial period and European indology owes a lot to the frequent contacts with the pandits whose help was necessary for the elucidation of so many Sanskrit texts. There has come into being a collaboration which gives the traditional pandit the opportunity to spread his learning and to give himself a new orientation; to the westerner the means of approaching the India that lies below the surface. Indology has in this way become an international science which gives Sanskrit a new possibility of extending its influence. For on the one hand Sanskrit documents offer important matter to the anthropologist who seeks to take note of the characteristics of humanity as a whole and does not overlook the Indian component. Cultural modernism itself tries to be universal, and to describe itself in all the cultural components of humanity, Sanskrit, Chinese, Arabic, just as much as Greek and Latin. On the other hand Sanskrit is interesting as a language not only to the linguist, but also to the epistemologist or in a more general way the researcher in the field of the new cognitive sciences, for it is indeed a choice subject for the observation of the relationship between the thought process and the language, being an instrument conditioned by the pandits for the processes of the mind, a tool proven by centuries of effective use. Sanskrit is interesting for computer scientists who find in Pāṇini's grammar interesting models of procedures for the generation of language.

Indian nationalism, exacerbated by colonial rule, has been working since achieving the independence of the country to reaffirm the values of traditional culture. Sanskrit is what embodies best the unity of traditional Indian civilisation. There is therefore a very strong sentiment which underlies a will to revive this language. The teaching, study, and literary production have never been interrupted. Efforts are currently being multiplied in all directions to maintain, develop and renew them. Sanskrit is taught in secondary schools as an optional language, at the higher levels in a more advanced way and with a scientific orientation to philology, linguistics, etc. but also according to traditional methods, in the specialised state or private schools. There are several Sanskrit universities (Vārāṇasī, Purī, Tirupati, etc.) where a course of teaching in all the major subjects, including scientific, is available in Sanskrit. There are major centres of Sanskrit studies at the head of international research (Bhandarkar Oriental Research Institute of Pune, etc.). There are a large number of private initiatives aiming to recreate a living and popular use of Sanskrit (Viśva Saṃskṛta Pratiṣṭhāna of Vārāṇasī, etc.). Sanskrit is not excluded from the major media: there are television programmes in the form of plays, children's programmes, etc. entirely in Sanskrit; daily news bulletins in Sanskrit on the radio broadcast all over India; more than one hundred periodicals including a daily paper, and a monthly magazine for children, *Canda Māmā*, with a circulation of 4,500 copies. There exists a Sanskrit literary production which is growing from one year to the next, in the traditional genres, and in revolutionary avant-garde forms. An example of the popular variety is a trend in lyric poetry close to folklore and song which enjoys considerable success.

A language lives by the will of the people who use it. The traditional pandits of today are of course small in number, but they are present everywhere. Their circle continues to widen through the spirit of innovation of the milieus who claim a modern Indianness. Sanskrit is their instrument, for this language has shown itself capable of preserving itself, always adapting itself, always enriching itself.

BIBLIOGRAPHY

BLOCH, J.; *L'Indo-aryen, du Véda aux temps modernes*, Paris, Maisonneuve, 1934.

CAILLAT, C., edited by; *Dialectes dans les littératures indo-aryennes*, Paris, Institut de Civilisation Indienne, 1989.

CARDONA, G.; *Pāṇini, a Survey of Research*, Delhi, Motilal Banarsidass, 1980.

FILLIOZAT, P.-S.; *Grammaire sanscrite pâninéenne*, Paris, Picard, 1988.

HAUDRY, J.; *L'Indo-européen*, 'Que sais-je', No.1798, Paris, P.U.F., 1979.

MOOKERJI, R.K.; *Ancient Indian Education*, Delhi, Motilal Banarsidass, 6th edition,1989.

PĀṆINI; *La Grammaire*, Sanskrit text with French translation by L. Renou, Paris, École Francaise d'Extrême-Orient, 2 vol., 1966.

PATAÑJALI; *Le Mahābhāṣya avec le Pradīpa de Kaiyaṭa et l'Uddyota de Nāgeśa*, French translation by P.-S. Filliozat, Pondicherry, Institut Français d'Indologie, 5 vol., published in 1975, 1976, 1978, 1980, 1986.

RENOU, L.; *Grammaire de la langue védique*, Lyon-Paris, IAC, 1952.

RENOU, L.; *Histoire de la langue sanscrite*, Lyon-Paris, IAC, 1956.

RENOU, L.; *Grammaire sanscrite*, Paris, Maisonneuve, 2nd edition, 1968.

RUEGG, D.-S.; *Contributions à l'histoire de la philosophie linguistique indienne*, Paris, Institut de Civilisation Indienne, 1959.

Other books of related interest
published by **Indica Books**:

- **A Concise Dictionary of Indian Philosophy**
  Sanskrit Terms Defined in English
  by John Grimes

- **Veda Samhitas**
  Rigveda, Yajurveda, Sama Veda, Atharvaveda
  Sanskrit text and English translation

- **Tarkabhasa: Exposition of Reasoning**
  by Kesava Misra, tr. by Ganganath Jha

- **A History of Pali Literature**
  by Bimala Churn Law